SRI LANKA

WAR-TORN ISLAND

SRI LANKA

WAR-TORN ISLAND

by Lawrence J. Zwier

Lerner Publications Company / Minneapolis

Website address: www.lernerbooks.com

All maps by Philip Schwartzberg, Meridian Mapping, Minneapolis.
Cover photo by Reuters/Corbis-Bettmann.
Table of contents photos (from top to bottom) by Reuters/Anuruddha
Lokuhapuarachchi/Archive Photos; The Illustrated London News Picture
Library; UPI/Corbis-Bettmann; CICR/Jean-P. Widmer.

Series Consultant: Andrew Bell-Fialkoff
Editor: Lori Coleman
Editorial Director: Mary M. Rodgers
Designer: Michael Tacheny
Photo Researcher: Gia Garbinsky

LIBRARY OF CONGRESS CATALOGING-IN-PUBLICATION DATA

Zwier, Lawrence J.
    Sri Lanka : War-torn island / by Lawrence J. Zwier.
        p. cm. — (World in conflict)
    Includes bibliographical references and index.
    Summary: A history of the ethnic conflict on Sri Lanka, including current issues.
    ISBN 0-8225-3550-5 (lib. bdg. : alk. paper)
    1. Sri Lanka—Ethnic relations—Juvenile literature. 2. Sri Lanka—Politics and government—
1978—Juvenile literature. 3. Tamil (Indic people)—Sri Lanka—Politics and government—
Juvenile literature.   [1. Sri Lanka—Ethnic relations. 2. Sri Lanka—Politics and government.]
I. Title. II. Series.
DS489.2.z95   1998
305.8'0095493-dc20
                                                                        96-24898

Manufactured in the United States of America
1 2 3 4 5 6 – JR – 03 02 01 00 99 98

CONTENTS

About the Series 6
Words You Need to Know 7
Foreword 8

INTRODUCTION 10
Terrain & Rainfall 10
Administrative Divisions
   & Cities 13
Ethnicity, Language,
   & Religion 13
Unclear Divisions 17
Who Lives Where.............17
Economic Activities 18
Major Players in
   the Conflict...................20

CHAPTER 1
THE RECENT CONFLICT AND ITS EFFECTS 22
Deep Trouble 25
An Internal War 28
Simpler, But Not Settled....30

CHAPTER 2
THE CONFLICT'S ROOTS 35
Europeans Arrive.............39
The British Period 40
Religious Revivals 46
Drive for Independence 48

CHAPTER 3
THE PRESENT CONFLICT 50
Trouble for Minorities 50
Early Ethnic Riots 53
The Jayewardene Years......56
From Bad to Worse............58
India Gets Involved 63
The JVP Resurfaces 67
The Tigers Claim Jaffna....69
Assassinations
   & Elections 72
The Talking Stops.............75
The Government
   Moves In 77

CHAPTER 4
WHAT'S BEING DONE TO SOLVE THE PROBLEM..........82
What the Government
   Can Do 82
Outside Pressure 85
Grassroots Efforts 86
Epilogue 90

Chronology 91
Selected Bibliography........93
Index..............................94
About the Author
   & Consultants 96

ABOUT THIS SERIES

Government firepower kills 25 protesters . . . Thousands of refugees flee the country . . . Rebels attack capital . . . Racism and rage flare . . . Fighting breaks out . . . Peace talks stall . . . Bombing toll rises to 52 . . . Slaughter has cost up to 50,000 lives.

Conflicts between people occur across the globe, and we hear about some of the more spectacular and horrific episodes in the news. But since most fighting doesn't directly affect us, we often choose to ignore it. And even if we do take the time to learn about these conflicts—from newspapers, magazines, television news, or radio—we're often left with just a snapshot of the conflict instead of the whole reel of film.

Most news accounts don't tell you the whole story about a conflict, focusing instead on the attention-grabbing events that make the headlines. In addition, news sources may have a preconceived idea about who is right and who is wrong in a conflict. The stories that result often portray one side as the "bad guys" and the other as the "good guys."

The *World in Conflict* series approaches each conflict with the idea that wars and political disputes aren't simply about bullies and victims. Conflicts are complex problems that can often be traced back hundreds of years. The people fighting one another have complicated reasons for doing so. Fighting erupts between groups divided by ethnicity, religion, and nationalism. These groups fight over power, money, territory, control. Sometimes people who just want to go about their own business get caught up in a conflict just because they're there.

These books examine major conflicts around the world, some of which are very bloody and others that haven't involved a lot of violence. They portray the people involved in and affected by conflicts. They describe how each conflict got started, how it developed, and where it stands. The books also outline some of the ways people have tried to end the conflicts. By reading the stories behind the headlines, you will learn some reasons why people hate and fight one another and, in addition, why some people struggle so hard to end conflicts.

WORDS YOU NEED TO KNOW

communalism: Loyalty to a sociopolitical group based on cultural and/or religious affiliation, with a primary emphasis on the promotion of that group's interests and culture.

devolution: The transference of power from a central authority to local governments.

embargo: A governmental decree prohibiting trade and transportation links to a particular place. An embargo is intended to warn or punish a particular group or to force by economic means an adversary to comply with the government's wishes.

ethnic group: A permanent group of people bound together by a combination of cultural markers, which may include—but are not limited to—race, nationality, tribe, religion, language, customs, and historical origins.

federalism: A distribution of power in government in which there exists a central authority and a number of subunits that surrender individual sovereignty but retain limited territorial control.

guerrilla: A rebel fighter, usually not associated with an internationally recognized government, who engages in irregular warfare. Membership in a guerrilla group usually indicates radical, aggressive, or unconventional activities.

nationalism: A feeling of loyalty or patriotism toward one's nation, with a primary emphasis on the promotion of a national culture and national interests.

paramilitary: Describing a supplementary fighting force.

quota: A set proportion or share allotted to a particular group. Ethnic quotas usually indicate how many jobs or opportunities are available to a certain ethnic group.

regional autonomy: The right and power of a region—usually characterized by a shared set of cultural markers, economy, and history—to govern itself.

secession: Formal withdrawal of an entity from a political unit, such as a nation, or from an organization, such as the United Nations, the North Atlantic Treaty Organization, or the European Union. The group seeking secession usually desires increased independence or autonomy.

separatist: An advocate of independence or autonomy for one's group. Separatists want representatives of their own group to make the political decisions that affect that group and wish to withdraw from any other political entity to which they're joined.

FOREWORD

by Andrew Bell-Fialkoff

Conflicts between various groups are as old as time. Peoples and tribes around the world have fought one another for thousands of years. In fact our history is in great part a succession of wars—between the Greeks and the Persians, the English and the French, the Russians and the Poles, and many others. Not only do states or ethnic groups fight one another, so do followers of different religions—Catholics and Protestants in Northern Ireland, Christians and Muslims in Bosnia, and Buddhists and Hindus in Sri Lanka. Often ethnicity, language, and religion—some of the main distinguishing elements of culture—reinforce one another in characterizing a particular group. For instance, the vast majority of Greeks are Orthodox Christian and speak Greek; most Italians are Roman Catholic and speak Italian. Elsewhere, one cultural aspect predominates. Serbs and Croats speak dialects of the same language but remain separate from one another because most Croats are Catholics and most Serbs are Orthodox Christians. To those two groups, religion is more important than language in defining culture.

We have witnessed an increasing number of conflicts in modern times—why? Three reasons stand out. One is that large empires—such as Austria-Hungary, Ottoman Turkey, several colonial empires with vast holdings in Asia, Africa, and America, and, most recently, the Soviet Union—have collapsed. A look at world maps from 1900, 1950, and 1998 reveals an ever-increasing number of small and medium-sized states. While empires existed, their rulers suppressed many ethnic and religious conflicts. Empires imposed order, and local resentments were mostly directed at the central authority. Inside the borders of empires, populations were multiethnic and often highly mixed. When the empires fell apart, world leaders found it impossible to establish political frontiers that coincided with ethnic boundaries. Different groups often claimed territories inhabited by others. The nations created on the lands of a toppled empire were saddled with acute border and ethnic problems from their very beginnings.

The second reason for more conflicts in modern times stems from the twin ideals of freedom and equality. In the United States, we usually think of freedom as "individual freedom." If we all have equal rights, we are free. But if you are a member of a minority group and feel that you are being discriminated against, your group's rights and freedoms are also important to you. In fact, if you don't have your "group freedom," you don't have full individual freedom either.

After World War I (1914–1918), the allied western nations, under the guidance of U.S. president Woodrow Wilson, tried to satisfy group rights by promoting minority rights. The spread of frantic nationalism in the 1930s, especially among disaffected ethnic minorities, and the catastrophe of World War II (1939–1945) led to a fundamental reassessment of the Wilsonian philosophy. After 1945 group rights were downplayed on the assumption that guaranteeing individual rights would be sufficient. In later decades, the collapse of multiethnic nations like Czechoslovakia, Yugoslavia, and the Soviet Union—coupled with the spread of nationalism in those regions—came as a shock to world leaders. People want democracy and individual rights, but they want their group rights, too. In practice, this means more conflicts and a cycle of secession, as minority ethnic groups seek their own sovereignty and independence.

The fires of conflict are often further stoked by the media, which lavishes glory and attention on independence movements. To fight for freedom is an honor. For every Palestinian who has killed an Israeli, there are hundreds of Kashmiris, Tamils, and Bosnians eager to shoot at their enemies. Newspapers, television and radio news broadcasts, and other media play a vital part in fomenting that sense of honor. They magnify each crisis, glorify rebellion, and help to feed the fire of conflict.

The third factor behind increasing conflict in the world is the social and geographic mobility that modern society enjoys. We can move anywhere we want and can aspire—or so we believe—to be anything we wish. Every day the television tantalizingly dangles the prizes that life can offer. We all want our share. But increased mobility and ambition also mean increased competition, which leads to antagonism. Antagonism often fastens itself to ethnic, racial, or religious differences. If you are an inner-city African American and your local grocer happens to be Korean American, you may see that individual as different from yourself—an intruder—rather than as a person, a neighbor, or a grocer. This same feeling of "us" versus "them" has been part of many an ethnic conflict around the world.

Many conflicts have been contained—even solved—by wise, responsible leadership. But unfortunately, many politicians use citizens' discontent for their own ends. They incite hatred, manipulate voters, and mobilize people against their neighbors. The worst things happen when neighbor turns against neighbor. In Bosnia, in Rwanda, in Lebanon, and in countless other places, people who had lived and worked together and had even intermarried went on a rampage, killing, raping, and robbing one another with gusto. If the appalling carnage teaches us anything, it is that we should stop seeing one another as hostile competitors and enemies and accept one another as people. Most importantly, we should learn to understand why conflicts happen and how they can be prevented. That is why *World in Conflict* is so important—the books in this series will help you understand the history and inner dynamics of some of the most persistent conflicts of modern times. And understanding is the first step to prevention. ⊕

INTRODUCTION

Sri Lanka is a tear-shaped tropical island nation in the Indian Ocean, just southeast of India. In fact, the northwestern tip of Sri Lanka's main island is only about 50 miles from the Indian mainland. Some very small sandbars belonging to Sri Lanka lie just a stone's throw away from similar shoals belonging to India. With a total land area of 25,332 square miles, Sri Lanka is about the size of the state of West Virginia and a bit smaller than the Republic of Ireland. The formal name of the country is the Democratic Socialist Republic of Sri Lanka.

Since the early 1980s, a bloody ethnic and political conflict has killed tens of thousands of Sri Lankans, forced more than half a million from their homes, ruined businesses, destroyed property on a massive scale, and consumed huge amounts of money. This war has also diverted the energies of a potentially productive country and has made everyday life a dangerous gamble.

TERRAIN & RAINFALL

The landscapes of Sri Lanka range from sandy beaches to cool, forested mountains. The hook-shaped Jaffna Peninsula in the north is a long, low-lying arm of limestone, with a large supply of fresh water in an underground aquifer. Most of Sri Lanka is fringed by a low coastal plain that meets the sea with palm-lined sandy beaches. At many points, the coastline is indented by narrow, shallow lagoons and lined by long, narrow barrier islands. A few excellent natural harbors—including one of the world's best at Trincomalee on the eastern coast—have long attracted seagoing traders to Sri Lanka.

The highest mountains lie in the south-central part of the island. The tallest is Pidurutalagala at 8,281 feet. Another of Sri Lanka's highest peaks is more famous—largely because of a footprint-like formation near its summit. Some claim the mark was left by the biblical figure Adam, and others attribute it to Buddha, the founder of the Buddhist religion. This well-known spot is Adam's Peak (also called Sri Pada), which reaches 7,360 feet.

The small tropical island of Sri Lanka has been anything but quiet and tranquil over the past decade. Fighting has mostly affected the capital, Colombo, and the Jaffna Peninsula, although violence has touched almost every part of the country.

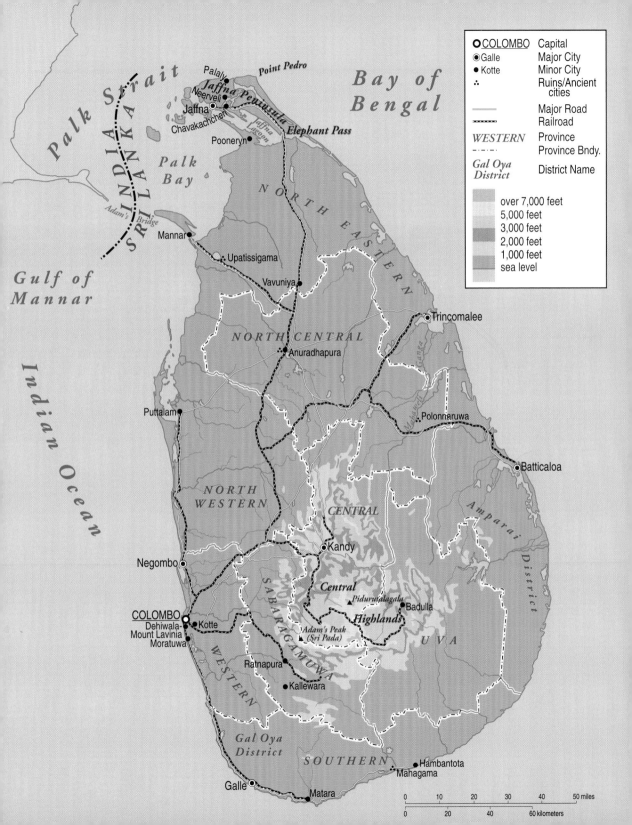

Palk Strait

Point Pedro

Bay of
Bengal

INDIA

SRI LANKA

Palaly
Jaffna
Neerveli
Jaffna
Chavakachcheri
Jaffna Peninsula
Jaffna Lagoon
Elephant Pass

Pooneryn

Palk
Bay

Adam's
Bridge

Mannar

Gulf of
Mannar

Upatissigama

Vavuniya

NORTH EASTERN

Trincomalee

NORTH CENTRAL

Anuradhapura

Puttalam

Polonnaruwa

Mahaweli Ganga

Batticaloa

NORTH
WESTERN

Indian Ocean

CENTRAL

Kandy

Negombo

Central

Amparai
District

SABARAGAMUWA

Pidurutalagala

Badulla

COLOMBO
Dehiwala-
Mount Lavinia
Moratuwa

Kotte

Highlands

UVA

Adam's Peak
(Sri Pada)

Ratnapura

WESTERN

Kallewara

Gal Oya
District

SOUTHERN

Hambantota
Mahagama

Galle

Matara

0   10   20   30   40   50 miles
0   20   40   60 kilometers

Plentiful rainfall in the central highlands nourishes lush greenery and vast crops of tea. Adam's Peak rises in the background.

soon blows from December to March, but the total precipitation this monsoon produces is only about 48 to 76 inches each year.

These rainfall patterns have created two main climatic zones in Sri Lanka—the Wet Zone in the southwestern quarter of the island and the Dry Zone elsewhere. Most of Sri Lanka's people live in the Wet Zone, but much of the Dry Zone of the north and east has traditionally been the homeland of ethnic Tamils. The Sinhalese people, however, nostalgically think of Dry Zone farming—practiced in the ancient kingdoms, with a town cooperatively organized around a "tank" (reservoir) and an irrigation system—as a high point of their civilization. Recent efforts by the government to move more Sinhalese farmers into the Dry Zone have angered longtime Tamil residents of these areas and have contributed to the conflict in Sri Lanka.

Both of these mountains are part of a system of ranges and plateaus that form the central highlands. A smaller area of rugged highlands and deep gorges—the Knuckles Massif—lies northeast of the central highlands, across a broad valley through which Sri Lanka's longest river, the Mahaweli Ganga, flows.

The high country defines rainfall patterns in Sri Lanka. Two monsoons (moist seasonal winds) affect the island, and the wetter of the

two blows from the southwest between mid-May and mid-October. When the moist air hits Sri Lanka's mountains and is forced upward, heavy rain—100 inches per year or more—falls in the southwestern and south-central areas of the country. By the time the airflow clears the mountains and reaches northern and eastern Sri Lanka, it has very little moisture to release. The north and the east receive the most rain when the northeast mon-

ADMINISTATIVE DIVISIONS & CITIES

Sri Lanka is divided into eight provinces: North-Eastern, North Central, Northwestern, Central, Uva, Western, Sabaragamuwa, and Southern. The provinces are in turn divided into 25 smaller administrative districts.

The largest city in Sri Lanka is Colombo, located on the populous southwestern coast, with a population of about 615,000. Another 460,000 people live in the nearby cities of Kotte, Dehiwala-Mount Lavinia, and Moratuwa. Colombo is the nation's center of business, finance, and—at least for now—government.

The Sri Lankan government is moving some of its offices to Sri Jayewardenapura, a part of Kotte, an ancient capital slightly southeast of Colombo. The district was designated the official administrative capital in 1982, but most departments continue to operate from Colombo.

Jaffna (population about 129,000) is the largest city in the north and a center of Tamil culture. Other significant cities and towns in Sri Lanka include Kandy (about 104,000 people), Galle (about 84,000), Trincomalee (about 47,000), and Batticaloa (about 45,000).

ETHNICITY, LANGUAGE, & RELIGION

Altogether about 18 million people live in Sri Lanka. They are broadly classified into a number of **ethnic groups,** the largest of which are the Sinhalese, the Tamils, and the Muslims.

The most numerous by far are the Sinhalese, who make up about 74 percent of the Sri Lankan population. Although the Sinhalese are an ethnic group, they are also a linguistic group. In general, one is considered Sinhalese if his or her native language is Sinhala. The language is closely related to several languages of northern India and distantly related to most European languages, including English. Despite belonging to such a far-flung family of languages, Sinhala is not widely spoken anywhere but in Sri Lanka. The Sinhalese identify themselves with a people who came to Sri Lanka from northern India about 2,500

Residents in Colombo wait in line for bread. Fighting in the capital has frequently closed down businesses and services such as gas, electricity, and water, causing shortages of food and other basic goods.

years ago, but the actual bloodlines of the modern Sinhalese trace back to many parts of India, not just the north.

Most of the Sinhalese (about 93 percent) profess the Buddhist religion, but several hundred thousand (especially in towns along the west coast) are Christians—mostly Roman Catholics or members of the Anglican-related Church of Ceylon. Most Sinhalese Buddhists believe Sri Lanka has a special place in worldwide Buddhism. Many think that the Buddha—an Indian philosopher named Siddhartha Gautama—actually set foot on the island in the fifth century B.C. In any case, most Sinhalese Buddhists see Sri Lanka as a kind of refuge for their religion. Buddhism had once been strong in India but had been largely displaced there by Hinduism by about A.D. 800.

Perhaps because they see the island as a haven for their religion, Sinhalese Buddhists have long insisted that the government protect and promote Buddhism. While the Sri Lankan constitution guarantees freedom of religion, it grants Buddhism the "foremost place" among the country's religions, an honor that angers Hindus, Muslims, and Christians alike.

The next most numerous people in Sri Lanka are the Tamils, with about 18 percent of the population. The Tamils are a distinct ethnic group who take their identity from a combination of linguistic and religious factors. In Sri Lanka, a Tamil is someone whose native language is Tamil and who is not a Muslim.

Tamil belongs to the Dravidian family of languages—

Buddha image in Sri Pushparam temple in Welithara

©Charles Walter Collection/Stock Montage, Inc.

The Buddhist faith in Sri Lanka takes a different form than in many other parts of Asia. Sri Lankan Buddhists—who follow the Theravada tradition instead of the more widespread Mahayana version—do not worship the Buddha but greatly respect him and his teachings. Sinhalese Buddhists consider it their duty to act as the protectors and custodians of the Buddhist relics, ancient written works, and forms of ritual and worship.

an entirely different family from that of Sinhala—and is spoken not only in Sri Lanka but in many parts of southern and southeastern Asia. In fact, it is used by more than 55 million people in southern India alone.

The Tamils of Sri Lanka—who first arrived about 2,000 years ago—rightly trace their ancestry to southern India, but this doesn't really distinguish them from other Sri Lankans. Many Sri Lankans who call themselves Sinhalese or Muslim, for example, also have south Indian ancestry.

People in an important subgroup of Tamils—called Indian Tamils or Estate Tamils—are numerous in the central highlands and in some coastal cities. Menial jobs, lower social status, and (for many of them) a different legal status separate these Indian Tamils from the Ceylon Tamils, whose families have longer histories of residence in Sri Lanka.

The government considers most Indian Tamils, who, beginning in the 1830s, were brought by British colonists to work on plantations, to be merely temporary workers on the island. This attitude

A Tamil worker picks tea leaves on a plantation in the central highlands. Tea plantations in the region have changed little over the decades and still employ mainly Indian Tamils (Estate Tamils) to work the fields.

even applies to Indian Tamils born in Sri Lanka, many of whom have never even been to India but whose parents had never become Sri Lankan citizens. Only about 25 percent of Sri Lanka's Indian Tamils have been granted Sri Lankan citizenship.

Most Tamils (just under 90 percent) follow the Hindu religion, but there are also some Christian Tamils, especially along the northwestern coast and near Jaffna. Both Hinduism and Buddhism originated in India. In Sri Lanka, the two religions have existed side by side for so long that they have greatly influenced one another. Some religious figures are worshiped in one form or another by both Hindus and Buddhists. In addition, the Hindu concept of caste has deeply influenced Buddhist society in Sri Lanka. (Caste is a social group, defined by social class or by the traditional occupation of one's family. Common examples in Sri Lanka are the "fishing" caste and the "cinnamon-peeling" caste.)

The third-largest group, with about 7 percent of Sri Lanka's population, are the Muslims (sometimes called Moors). The Muslims are a religious group, but they are also an ethnic group in Sri Lanka. Most Muslims speak Tamil but do not consider themselves Tamils because their religion, Islam, sets them apart. Islam came to Sri Lanka as the native religion of Arabs, north Indians, Malays, and other peoples who migrated to Sri Lanka beginning in the eighth century. The efforts of Muslim missionaries later expanded the number of Islamic followers.

The remaining 1 percent of the population consists of various peoples. A very small number are Veddas, descendants of a group that inhabited Sri Lanka even before the Sinhalese or the Tamils arrived. The rest are people of numerous European or Asian backgrounds—such as Dutch, Portuguese, British, Bengali, and Malay—many of whom have mixed ancestry.

Muslims in Colombo bow down in prayer in an open lot. Devout followers of the religion pray facing Mecca, a holy city in Saudi Arabia.

Some Sri Lankans are called Burghers, a term for people who are part Asian but also have significant European ancestry (usually Dutch or Portuguese) dating back to Sri Lanka's colonial days. This group remains very small (only about 39,000 people in the early 1980s) but was very influential in trade and politics when Sri Lanka was a British colony. The primary languages of these smaller minority groups include English, Portuguese, Malay, and Tamil. English, in fact, is the second language of many Sri Lankans.

UNCLEAR DIVISIONS
This portrait of the main communities in Sri Lanka is convenient, but it oversimplifies a very complicated situation. Not all Tamils—or all Sinhalese or all Muslims—have the same interests and want the same things. Smaller divisions defined by religion, language, length of residence in Sri Lanka, and caste create rifts within each larger group.

Roman Catholic Sinhalese have often been at odds with Buddhist Sinhalese. The same has been true of Christian and Hindu Tamils. Sinhalese of the Goyigama ("landowning") caste compete with Sinhalese of the Karava ("fishing") caste for prominence in government. Some Jaffna Tamils look down on East Coast Tamils, whom they stereotype as being unsophisticated and of lower caste. Kandyan Sinhalese from the central highlands sometimes feel culturally superior to Lowland Sinhalese, whom they consider tainted by centuries of contact with Europeans.

Sri Lankans can't usually tell just by looking at someone whether he or she is Sinhalese or Tamil or Muslim or even Burgher. Many Tamils have escaped harm during

WHO LIVES WHERE
The Sinhalese are a majority in Sri Lanka as a whole and in every individual province except for the North-Eastern. The Tamils, though a national minority, are a majority in the northern part of the country and make up nearly half of the population along sections of the eastern coast. This distribution has given the Tamils a geographical base during the country's conflict and has encouraged many Tamils to envision a separate Tamil nation in the north and east. The Muslims are not a majority in any region of Sri Lanka, but they do live in large concentrations in some parts of the northwest and the east.

Probably the most thor-

Not all Tamils—or all Sinhalese or all Muslims— have the same interests and want the same things.

---

anti-Tamil rioting by successfully pretending to be from some other ethnic group—and by speaking as little as possible. It's usually only after someone begins to speak that his or her ethnic group becomes apparent.

oughly mixed areas of the country are in the east, where many areas are about one-third Sinhalese, one-third Tamil, and one-third Muslim. This is partly because of a government program begun in the 1930s to colonize lightly populated parts of the country. Notably, this program has resettled many Sinhalese families in Dry Zone areas, where the majority of earlier residents were Tamils.

The ethnic conflict in Sri Lanka has altered the distribution of the population throughout the island. Because Tamil rebels are in control of many areas of the north, almost no Sinhalese live in such cities as Jaffna. Similarly, very few Tamils live in conservative Sinhalese Buddhist areas in the Southern Province. Riots in 1983 caused many of Colombo's prosperous Tamils to flee to Tamil-dominated parts of the north and east, thereby increasing already-strong Tamil majorities in these areas.

Fishers haul in their catch after returning to the lagoon near Negombo, a west-coast town north of Colombo.

ECONOMIC ACTIVITIES

About half of Sri Lanka's workers are employed in agriculture. The country is the world's number-one exporter of tea, which is grown mostly on vast plantations in the central highlands. Rubber and coconut, also raised chiefly on large plantations, are significant export crops as well. Although rice production is high, Sri Lankan rice paddies produce only about three-fourths as much as the country needs. Many Sri Lankans are also involved in fishing and in raising livestock, principally buffalo and cattle.

Sri Lanka has deposits of valuable minerals, including such gemstones as sapphires and rubies. More important are less glamorous minerals, such as graphite—used in the making of pencils and as a lubricant—and iron.

Sri Lanka's economy is not highly industrialized. Altogether, industry accounts for about 29 percent of economic production in Sri Lanka, and only about 19 percent of the Sri Lankan workforce has industrial jobs. Most of these jobholders manufacture clothing, process food, or work in construction.

The service sector—including banking, insurance sales, teaching, and government—is quite important in the Sri Lankan economy, accounting for just under half of the value of all the country's economic activity in recent years. Among Sri Lanka's greatest assets are a relatively well-educated population and a reasonably high rate of adult literacy (about 88 percent).

Unfortunately, the relatively high-quality education

Merchants in Colombo survey the damage done to their shops and businesses after a week of rioting. Racial riots, fires, and bombs have destroyed thousands of homes and businesses in the capital since the early 1980s.

available in Sri Lanka has produced more skilled workers than the nation's economy has been able to absorb. As a result, many Sri Lankan bankers, lawyers, teachers, engineers, and other professionals have left to find work in other countries—such as Malaysia, Singapore, the United Kingdom, the United States, and Canada—where their English-language abilities help them fit in. (English is widely spoken in Sri Lanka, especially among professional people.)

Sri Lankans also provide much of the skilled and unskilled labor in Kuwait, Saudi Arabia, Dubai, and other oil-rich nations on the Arabian Peninsula. Although these overseas workers send a lot of money back to their families in Sri Lanka, the continuing loss of talented and well-educated professionals poses a long-term threat to the national economy.

But perhaps the biggest drag on the Sri Lankan economy is the war. Not only has this ongoing conflict caused thousands of deaths and enormous destruction, it has cost billions of dollars to finance. As long as lives and resources are sacrificed to continue the fighting, Sri Lanka's future outlook remains grim. ⊕

MAJOR PLAYERS IN THE CONFLICT

Sirimavo Bandaranaike

SWRD Bandaranaike

Bandaranaike, Sirimavo Became prime minister upon the assassination of her husband, SWRD Bandaranaike, in 1959. She ruled from 1960 to 1965 and from 1970 to 1977.

Bandaranaike, SWRD Quit the United National Party and formed the Sri Lanka Freedom Party in 1951. He served as prime minister from 1956 to 1959.

Eelam National Democratic Liberation Front (ENDLF) A coalition of Tamil secessionist groups that joined forces in 1987. The group opposes the militant practices of the Liberation Tigers of Tamil Eelam. Many of its members fled to India when Indian troops withdrew from Sri Lanka in 1990.

Indian Peace-Keeping Force (IPKF) A military force sent from India to Sri Lanka in 1987. Its purpose was to disarm Tamil guerrillas and to help set up a new North-Eastern Province. The troops pulled out in 1990.

Janatha Vimukhti Peramuna (JVP, "People's Liberation Front") A militant Sinhalese movement against Tamil self-determination. The JVP was banned in 1971 after attempting to overthrow the government, but the group continued terroristic attacks against Tamils and government leaders until government security forces eliminated most JVP leaders in 1989.

Jayewardene, Junius Richard Leader of the United National Party who became prime minister in 1977. Later he became president and amended the constitution to stay in power for 11 years.

Junius R. Jayewardene

Kumaratunga, Chandrika Leader of the Sri Lanka Freedom Party who became president in 1994. She is the daughter of Sirimavo and SWRD Bandaranaike. Her late husband Vijaya Kumaratunga, led the SLFP until he was assassinated in 1988.

Chandrika Kumaratunga

Liberation Tigers of Tamil Eelam (LTTE, or Tamil Tigers) The most prominent militant secessionist Tamil group in Sri Lanka. The group has fought to establish a separate Tamil state in Sri Lanka since 1972.

Prabhakaran, Vellupillai Founder and leader of the Liberation Tigers of Tamil Eelam.

Premadasa, Ranasinghe Served as prime minister from 1978 to 1987 and became president in 1988. He negotiated the withdrawal of Indian troops in 1990.

Sri Lanka Freedom Party (SLFP) Founded in 1951 by SWRD Bandaranaike. Advocating a "Sinhala-only" party platform, the SLFP first came to power in 1956.

Vellupillai Prabhakaran

Tamil United Front (TUF) An alliance of moderate Tamil groups that came together in 1972. In May 1976 the alliance changed its name to the *Tamil United Liberation Front* (TULF) and officially called for a separate Tamil state of Eelam.

United National Party (UNP) Political party founded in 1946 by Don Stephen Senanayake, Ceylon's (Sri Lanka's) first prime minister after independence.

Ranasinghe Premadasa

CHAPTER

1

THE RECENT CONFLICT AND ITS EFFECTS

Imagine a 15-year-old boy named Raj, a Tamil who lives in a refugee camp in the northern part of the Jaffna Peninsula. His real home is in the city of Jaffna, but his family members—like almost everyone else in Jaffna—had to abandon their home and most of their possessions as the Sri Lankan army advanced on the city in late 1995. The last thing the local people wanted was to be caught in the army's street-by-street, house-by-house battle to recapture Jaffna from Tamil rebels.

Raj wants to visit his cousins in a town to the southeast called Vavuniya. They don't live very far away—only about 60 miles—but Raj's trip won't be easy. Raj's parents say good-bye and wish him luck, somewhat worried for their son's safety. Still, Jaffna has been a war zone ever since

Raj was born, and he has grown used to difficulty. In Jaffna, if you do only what's easy and perfectly safe, you'll never do anything at all.

Before he can leave the camp, Raj needs to get permission from the Liberation Tigers of Tamil Eelam (LTTE), the armed rebel group that was long the unofficial government of Jaffna and that has watchful representatives in all the refugee camps. The Tamil Tigers (as the rebel group is also known) question him thoroughly about where he wants to go and why. Raj worries that they will not let him leave. Having lost a lot of fighters lately, Tiger commanders are desperate for new recruits of just about Raj's age. If they do let him leave, they will make sure Raj's brother or some other close relative remains in the camp while he's gone. If Raj

does anything to anger the Tigers, it could spell trouble for his family.

After leaving the camp, Raj has to find some form of transportation. Even if he could make his way to a bus station, there wouldn't be any buses running from the peninsula to Vavuniya. The only road is blocked at Elephant Pass, the narrow point where the Jaffna Peninsula joins the main part of the island. It's a double blockade—guarded on the south side by Sri Lankan soldiers enforcing the government's anti-Tiger **embargo** and on the north by the Tigers, who are trying to keep supplies from reaching the government forces on the peninsula. The train that used to run from Colombo to Jaffna hasn't traveled north of Vavuniya since the late 1980s. There's nowhere for it to go—at least not beyond the Elephant Pass blockade.

Raj figures that his best bet is to get to a jetty (landing wharf) and take a boat southward across the narrow Jaffna Lagoon to one of the villages on the main part of the island. Even though the government sometimes bans civilian traffic across the lagoon, the bans are not always enforced. It's a short crossing, and the boats there have been free from attack by the Tamil **guerrillas.**

Raj finds a fisherman willing to take a few passengers across for five rupees each (about one dollar), so Raj pays him and climbs aboard the small, brightly painted wooden boat. When the sun gets hot, Raj sometimes ducks inside the boat's tiny cabin, a simple shedlike enclosure just big enough for two or three people to huddle inside. But most of the time he enjoys being on deck—watching the other boats, feeling the salt breeze, listening to the boat's small engine chug along, and enjoying the strong smells of the lagoon's muddy shore.

Once he has landed, Raj thinks about renting a bicycle and pedaling the remaining distance to Vavuniya. But that would mean a couple of days of hot, hard riding and—in the northeast monsoon season—a very wet trip. He decides instead to hitch a ride by truck or van to Vavuniya. He finds a Tamil man whose battered blue pickup has a bed full of vegetables and an empty seat up front. The man would rather have a strong passenger like Raj on board in case the truck bogs down on a bad road, so he agrees to give him a ride. They set off in the midafternoon heat as thunderclouds gather. Raj is glad he decided against the bike.

The ride winds through some lonely stretches of scrub jungle, perfect territory for an ambush, but Raj isn't very worried. He has his pass from the Tigers, and they control the roads north of Vavuniya. Unless his driver strays too near the military base at Pooneryn, they will probably not come across any government checkpoints—and that's good for Raj. At government barricades, the soldiers (almost all of whom are Sinhalese) would probably suspect any young Tamil of being a rebel. Given the slightest excuse, they might arrest him—or simply drag him out of public view and shoot him.

At one time, before the Tamil Tigers frightened most Sinhalese colonists away from Vavuniya, an overland trip through this area would have been very dangerous. Raj could have easily been caught up in a local blood feud—the sort of violence still common farther south and east near Batticaloa and Amparai. Here's the usual scenario: the Tamil Tigers attack Sinhalese or Muslims, an angry mob goes looking for Tamils, and one person is killed to avenge the death of another. In conditions like these, many an innocent Sri Lankan on an unremarkable

Here's the usual scenario: the Tamil Tigers attack Sinhalese or Muslims, an angry mob goes looking for Tamils, and one person is killed to avenge the death of another.

trip has been pulled from a car or bus and beaten or hacked to death.

Along the road, Raj keeps an eye on the jungle and on the roadbed. He knows that absolute silence one minute can be followed by vicious fighting or a bomb blast the next. Raj remarks to the driver that he's glad he's visiting his Vavuniya relatives and not the ones in the east, near Batticaloa. The driver agrees. He says he tries to steer clear of "Batti" and its travel hazards—sniper fire from the jungle, exploding mines or crossfire between the rebels and the troops. At least for the time being, the northern Vanni—the area north of Vavuniya—is relatively safe.

When the truck finally reaches Vavuniya, the sun is setting and the streets are coming to life for the evening. Hawkers set up food stalls and market vendors lay out plastic utensils and aluminum pots for sale. Portable generators are sputtering to life to power the fluorescent lights of roadside restaurants, and boom boxes are alive with hit tunes from Tamil movies. The driver lets Raj out along the main road, only a few blocks from his cousins' house. After running most of the way to the modest cinderblock home on a dusty sidestreet, he is eagerly welcomed by his aunt and uncle and cousins. His journey is over.

But during his short visit, he contemplates what awaits him. Vavuniya is safe for now, but what will happen in the next few days? He might have to take an entirely different route home, if fighting has erupted again along once-calm roads. He cannot even be sure his family will be waiting for him at the same camp he left, since new battles might have forced the refugees to move elsewhere. Will he ever return to his home in Jaffna, to sleep again in his room? That depends on what happened when the troops went in to clear out the Tigers. How important was his street, his house, even his room in the battle for Jaffna? For all he knows, there may be no house to go back to.

DEEP TROUBLE

Raj's difficulties in visiting his cousins are symptoms of deep trouble in one of the most beautiful places on earth. In news reports throughout the world, the name Sri Lanka—once associated with stunning scenery and high cultural achievements—is almost always linked with battles, bombings, assassinations, and death.

Examples of the violence that has occurred in Sri Lanka are jarring. In October 1994, more than 50 Sri Lankans—including Gamini Dissanayake, one of the leading candidates for president—were killed in an

Toppled chairs clutter the site of the October 1994 bombing that killed Gamini Dissanayake, a candidate for president. Dissanayake, pictured on the poster, was speaking at a political rally when a suicide bomber detonated the powerful explosives.

A government soldier loads a mortar shell near the city of Jaffna. Sri Lankan military forces revved up efforts to take the city—a Tamil Tiger stronghold—in 1995 and eventually succeeded in driving the rebel forces out.

explosion at an election rally in the suburbs of Colombo. A young woman seen reaching up under her T-shirt just before the blast was probably pressing the detonator of a powerful bomb strapped to her body. The bomb was loaded with ball bearings to make it more deadly. The woman's head was later found on top of a building 80 yards away.

The explosion was widely assumed to be the work of the Tamil Tigers. The LTTE

and other Tamil rebel groups want Tamil-dominated parts of Sri Lanka to break away and create a separate Tamil nation—Eelam—in the north and east.

In April 1995, Sea Tigers—scuba divers from the LTTE—attached bombs to the hulls of two gunboats belonging to the Sri Lankan navy. Shortly thereafter, explosions ripped through Trincomalee harbor, destroying the ships and killing 12 sailors. Peace talks between the government and the rebels—which had brought more than three months of calm to a war-weary country—fell apart. In the following six months, at least 4,000 people died in a rapidly escalating war.

In May 1995, Tamil Tiger commandos slipped into Kallawara, a fishing village near Trincomalee, and massacred 42 villagers. While the rebels hacked their victims to death, another group of Tigers set fire to a nearby army outpost so the soldiers could not go to the aid of the villagers.

Two months later, government forces, planning to retake rebel-held towns on the Jaffna Peninsula, dropped leaflets warning civilians of the operation. The leaflets advised people to take shelter in churches and temples, but a government jet flying over the town of Navali dropped nine bombs on the Roman Catholic Church of Saints Peter and Paul. The bombs killed 62 people who had huddled there for safety and seriously wounded many others.

In September 1995, the Sri Lankan police admitted that 21 mutilated bodies dis-

© Dexter Cruez/Sygma

LTTE suicide bombers targeted the capital's main gasoline depot in October 1995, blowing up storage tanks that burned for four days.

covered near Colombo were those of men killed while being detained by the Special Task Force (STF). The STF is a paramilitary police unit trained by former commandos of the British Special Air Service and assigned to combat the Tamil Tigers. The STF had apparently starved or strangled the men to death and then mutilated their bodies to make them hard to identify.

In October 1995, about 25,000 government troops closed in on Jaffna city, which they eventually captured from the Tamil Tigers. Ahead of the army advance, at least 100,000—and maybe as many as 500,000—people fled from their homes and joined an already-huge group of Sri Lankans—Tamils, Sinhalese, and Muslims—who are homeless refugees in their own country.

In the same month, Tamil Tiger commandos disguised as government soldiers blew up most of the mammoth oil-storage tanks at two depots just outside Colombo. Firefighters worked for four days to put out the flames, which rained soot on the capital and reminded Sri Lankans that the war is not limited to the north and east. The rebels caused at least $61 million worth of damage in this one incident. Luckily, the fires were put out before they could spread through fuel pipes to the center of Colombo.

Late in January 1996, suicide bombers—presumed to be Tamil Tigers—drove a truck packed with explosives into the front entrance of the Central Bank building in downtown Colombo. Nearly 1,500 people were injured by the huge blast, and at least 85 were killed. Colombo residents found their city the new focus of destruction as the Tigers—ousted nearly three months earlier from their headquarters in Jaffna—kept up pressure on the government.

In July 1996, a Tamil suicide bomber crashed into a motorcade of government of-

Workers in Colombo's commercial district flee the area after a bomb blast in January 1996.

ficials in Jaffna, wounding 60 people and killing 23 others—including the Jaffna city commander, Major General Ananda Hamangoda. The attack, which occurred as the Sri Lankan government was planning reconstruction efforts on the peninsula, likely dissuaded some foreign-aid donors Sri Lanka was counting on for assistance in the rehabilitation project.

AN INTERNAL WAR

This small sampling of incidents only hints at the death and destruction Sri Lanka has suffered, mostly because of an intense internal war between the government's security forces and some well-armed Tamil rebels. These rebels, most prominently the LTTE, are **separatists.** Decades of discrimination and anti-Tamil violence have convinced them that they can never enjoy equal status with the Sinhalese in a united country. The Tamil Tigers and other rebel groups want to run Eelam, the Tamil-dominated nation they propose, without Sinhalese interference.

Not every separatist believes in using violence to win independence, and not every Tamil is a separatist. But many are. Most Tamils who are not separatists hope for some sort of Tamil autonomy (self-rule) without completely breaking away from Sri Lanka.

Almost every Sinhalese opposes the division of the island. Moderate Sinhalese oppose **secession** but are willing to allow the Tamils some autonomy in Tamil-

How can a small rebel group like the Tamil Tigers continue to wage war against the Sri Lankan government forces? The government has an 80,000-member army, which continues to expand, a 50,000-member police force responsible for internal security, and a 5,000-member Home Guard in charge of protecting Muslim and Sinhalese communities in and near the war zone. In addition, the government equips Tamil militias opposed to the LTTE.

The Tamil Tigers, with a 10,000-member militia, are always actively recruiting additional soldiers. The Tigers raise money for their cause from Tamil immigrants in Australia, Britain, and Germany. Until the late 1980s, the LTTE enjoyed the support of the Indian government, which provided training camps in southern India and supplied arms to the militia. Some observers say that the strong leadership of Vellupillai Prabhakaran is one of the reasons for the group's endurance. Whatever the secret behind their ability to survive, the Tamil Tigers won't give up their cause easily.

Tamil Tiger flag

Artwork by: John Este

majority regions. This position—no secession but some self-government—is the one favored by the government of Sri Lanka's president, Chandrika Kumaratunga. More extreme Sinhalese don't support the president's point of view. They claim Sri Lanka's destiny is to be wholly Sinhalese and wholly Buddhist, and they are unwilling to concede anything that might weaken the influence of Sinhalese Buddhism.

Sri Lanka's Muslims and members of other minorities are in an awkward position. Like the Tamils, they have been discriminated against under a system that favors Sinhalese Buddhists, but a lot of them see no point in separating from Sri Lanka only to become a minority in a new Tamil nation.

The conflict in Sri Lanka is an internal ethnic, religious, and political war in which the combatants are all native to Sri Lanka. The conflict is partly about secession, but at a more basic level—and for a much longer time—it has been a struggle to define the relationships among various ethnic groups in a small country with limited resources.

Before the conflict flared up in the early 1980s, some Muslims felt a kinship with the Tamils, because both minority groups lived in a nation monopolized by Sinhalese. Yet most Muslims consider themselves quite distinct. And in the 1980s and 1990s, Tamil Tiger attacks on Muslim villages in the east led Muslims there to assert their desire to be excluded from a Tamil-dominated North-Eastern Province. Many Muslims would prefer to achieve automony apart from any settlement with the Tamils. In any case, Sri Lankan Muslims haven't allied themselves with any of the other ethnic groups on the island.

The battles in this war occur most frequently in northern Sri Lanka, especially on the Jaffna Peninsula, and in eastern districts like Batticaloa and Trincomalee. Bombings occur in Colombo. Very few parts of the country have been untouched by violence.

The fighting in the north is sometimes an organized type of warfare with battle lines and fortifications. This kind of warfare often occurs when government troops try to reoccupy land where the Tamil Tigers have long been the only real power. In the east, any exchange of fire is usually in response to a sudden guerrilla strike by the Tigers against the government's naval base at Trincomalee or an attack on a military patrol, a police post,

or a vulnerable village full of Muslim or Sinhalese civilians.

Massacres of civilians usually occur in isolated fishing villages and in colonization zones like Amparai or Gal Oya—traditional Tamil homelands recently settled by Sinhalese. In Colombo suicide bombers have detonated explosives at political rallies, in crowded shopping districts, in government offices, and in train stations.

Most news reports speak of the civil war as having begun in 1983. A lot of serious violence occurred in Sri Lanka earlier than that, but 1983 was the year in which the previously sporadic outbreaks of violence came to look more like war. No one knows for sure how many Sri Lankans have died in this war—the lowest estimates are about 36,000, the highest around 50,000. In addition hundreds of thousands have been injured, and at least half a million have been forced to leave their homes as a result of the war.

SIMPLER, BUT NOT SETTLED

As knotty as Sri Lanka's problems are, they have been far more complex at other times. In the late 1980s, for example, the armed combatants in Sri Lanka included not only government soldiers and Tiger guerrillas but also about 60,000 government troops from India. Also involved in the fighting was a group of Sinhalese extremists called the Janatha Vimukthi Peramuna (JVP),

Sri Lankan president Junius R. Jayewardene (left) *met with Indian prime minister Rajiv Gandhi* (right) *in November 1987 to discuss an Indo-Sri Lankan agreement for negotiating peace in northern and eastern Sri Lanka.*

Police officers stand guard while investigators dig up a mass grave near Suriyakande. The grave is believed to contain the remains of JVP members killed by the Sri Lankan military in 1989.

Reuters/Anuruddha Lokuhapuarachchi/Archive Photos

which means People's Liberation Front. In addition various Tamil separatist militants were competing with the Tigers for dominance, and unofficial death squads were hired by the government to eliminate rebels of all types.

The Indian soldiers pulled out of Sri Lanka in early 1990. Although there are still dangerous Sinhalese extremists in the country, they have not been responsible for any large-scale killing since the government crushed the JVP in late 1989. Even the rival groups of Tamil militants, once famous for spectacular battles among themselves in Sri Lanka and in India, rarely exchange fire anymore.

The government's security forces—including the army, the navy, the police, and some less organized, minimally trained forces known as Home Guards—concentrate on one main opponent, the Tigers. But that hasn't ensured success, especially since few clear battle lines exist in a guerrilla war. Even as the army bore down on Tiger strongholds in the north in 1995 and 1996, Tiger guerrillas struck near Colombo and in the east. The frustrated security forces—protected somewhat by laws that permit rough handling of the rebels—have often gone too far, harassing Tamil youths, raiding villages, and apprehending young Tamils who are either never heard from again or turn up dead.

Although fewer groups are fighting in the 1990s than in the 1980s, Sri Lanka's ethnic war seems no closer to being resolved. If anything, the Tamil Tigers are better armed than ever—and less willing to negotiate peace.

CHAPTER 1   *The Recent Conflict and Its Effects*

They have accurate surface-to-air missiles that analysts didn't know about until the Tigers shot down two government transport planes near the Palaly airbase in April 1995. They have a navy, including an entire unit of scuba divers who carry out repeated seaborne operations against the government. The Tigers also have what may be the world's only guerrilla air force, with airstrips and ultralight aircraft. At one point in September 1995, the government was so worried by rumors that the Tigers were planning an air attack on the capital that all domestic flights were canceled.

A Tamil Tiger fighter aims before shooting a rocket-propelled grenade in the war-torn Jaffna Peninsula.

The Sri Lankan government, which spent at least $500 million on new military hardware in late 1995, seemed more determined than ever to settle the country's problems by force—or at least batter the Tigers enough to force them into negotiations. This is an expensive course of action.

According to President Kumaratunga, the Sri Lankan government spent about $320 million on the war effort from mid-April to mid-October of 1995 alone. That figure averages out to about $1.75 million each day.

Although the president came to power in late 1994 with hopes of negotiating peace, the Tigers walked out of the talks she initiated. Sinhalese extremists, including influential organizations of Buddhist monks, clamor for the complete military defeat

In 1995 Sri Lanka's defense budget was 29.4 billion rupees (about $600 million)—5.6 percent of the nation's GDP (gross domestic product, or the total monetary value of goods and services produced in the country in a year). The budget for 1996 expanded military spending. Continued fighting during that year increased the amount of military spending that was forecast earlier. Despite the enormous amount of money the government has spent on the war against the LTTE, Sri Lanka's economy continues to grow.

of the Tamil rebels. Even the hint of a negotiated settlement raises threats that radical Sinhalese forces will paralyze the country with strikes and assassinations as the JVP did in the late 1980s. Peace in Sri Lanka seems very far away.

Because distrust runs deep among Sri Lankans of different backgrounds, it's easy to believe—as do many ethnic extremists on the island—that the modern combatants are just playing out a centuries-old conflict. History doesn't necessarily support this view, but history is where Sri Lanka's modern problems are indeed rooted. It is a history often rewritten, often manipulated, often mixed with half-truths and legends, and often used to justify terror and oppression. ⊕

The Disappeared

The disappearances of Sri Lankans abducted by death squads are a festering national wound that has to be tended to. In 1991 the Mother's Front, a group of relatives of the disappeared, began rallying to demand explanations from government officials. Amnesty International, a global human-rights organization, has kept records of disappearances. The group is pressing for full investigations and punishment of those found guilty of the murders. More than 34,000 disappearance cases have been brought up for investigation.

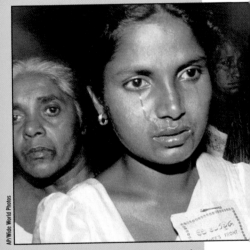

The Mothers' Front was inaugurated in 1991 to call attention to the disappearances of tens of thousands of people in 1989 and 1990.

The pretext for the murders was the elimination of the JVP, but the politicians who controlled the death squads probably also used the opportunity to settle grudges and to get rid of legitimate political opponents. For example, one mass grave discovered in January 1994 contained the bodies of perhaps 200 death-squad victims, probably including 20 or 30 high school students. Some reports claim that the students had been killed because a politically powerful high school principal wanted to punish them for teasing his son. The case could not be thoroughly investigated because bulldozers tampered with the site even as police supposedly guarded it.

It is hard to get the police and the army to cooperate in investigating these disappearances because any honest investigation would surely implicate many of their members. The Kumaratunga government feels somewhat freer to pursue the cases than did the United National Party (the political party whose members controlled the death squads), but the government remains reluctant to prosecute security personnel, who are needed to fight the Tamil rebels. Nevertheless, three inquiry commissions have been set up by the Kumaratunga government in different parts of Sri Lanka.

The Thupurama Dagoba, probably the oldest religious monument in Sri Lanka, was built by Devanampiyatissa around 300 B.C. The dagoba is said to contain the right collarbone of the Buddha.

CHAPTER 2

THE CONFLICT'S ROOTS

Both Sinhalese and Tamils have long lived on the island that is now Sri Lanka. The earliest Sinhalese probably arrived about 2,500 years ago. The first large groups of Tamils came at least 1,500 years ago, although smaller numbers had existed on the island probably as long as the early Sinhalese settlers. When the first Sinhalese arrived on the island, they found it populated by a group called the Veddas. Over time, the Veddas were pushed into remote territories or absorbed into the populations of the newcomers.

Sinhalese legends say that an Indian prince named Vijaya established the first Sinhalese kingdom on Sri Lanka after he and his followers landed on the western coast of the island. The day of their landing was supposedly the very day of the Buddha's death, in about 483 B.C. Vijaya had no son, so the rule of his kingdom eventually passed to his nephew, Panduvasaveda, who migrated from India and set up his court at a city called Upatissigama in the west-central part of the island.

These legends about Vijaya and his band of settlers don't record events exactly as they happened, but they most likely contain some elements of fact. There probably was a kingdom whose rulers spoke Sinhala (or a language close to it) at Upatissigama around the fifth century B.C. Not much later, the capital of this kingdom moved to Anuradhapura in north-central Sri Lanka.

Early chronicles of Sri Lankan history, written by Buddhist monks, are greatly concerned with explaining how Buddhism came to Sri Lanka. They claim that a son of the great Indian emperor Asoka was carried through the air to Sri Lanka, where he converted King Devanampiyatissa of Anuradhapura to the Buddhist religion. King Devanampiyatissa then set up Buddhist monasteries and ensured the whole island's conversion. In reality, however, the residents of Sri Lanka were probably converted much less miraculously by monks from India, sometime before 200 B.C.

By that time, Buddhist kings ruled several kingdoms in Sri Lanka. Anuradhapura was the strongest. Other less-powerful kingdoms existed east and south of the highlands, mostly in the valleys of the larger rivers. At this early stage, there were probably no Hindu kingdoms on the island yet.

Because modern Sri Lankans associate being Buddhist with being Sinhalese, the early Buddhist kingdoms are usually considered Sinhalese. But historians have become cautious about using modern ethnic terms to describe them. It is unlikely that the people of these kingdoms were all of one ethnic group or even that ethnic divisions meant much to them. The people were probably a lot more conscious of other differences within their societies—differences of class, family line, and occupation. Important conflicts in early Sri Lankan history were not between Sinhala speakers and Tamil speakers or even between Buddhists and Hindus, but between supporters

The Buddhist Chronicles

Curious about the people newly under their rule, British officials in the early 1800s discovered that Sri Lanka had a written history going back to nearly 500 B.C., recorded by Buddhist monks in various chronicles. The most important of these works is the *Mahavamsa,* the first installment of which was written in the fifth century A.D. by a monk named Mahanama. This first part of the *Mahavamsa,* written in Pali (a classical Asian language), covers events from the supposed arrival of Prince Vijaya up to about A.D. 300. In 1877 came the *Culavamsa,* a Sinhalese-language translation of the original *Mahavamsa* plus updates that brought the account up to 1815, the beginning of the British era. The narrative would later be updated in 1935 and again in 1978.

Because the *Mahavamsa* was written in Pali, few Sinhalese could read it until its translation. It was the British who made the *Mahavamsa* a widely distributed work, publishing an English translation of the first part of the *Mahavamsa* in 1837. The British governor also commissioned the 1877 Sinhalese translation of the original and its updates.

Ancient Sri Lankan cities were built with reservoirs, or tanks, ranging in size from 3,000 acres to the dimensions of a swimming pool. The large tanks provided water for irrigation, while the smaller ones were used as baths. This small tank, built over 2,000 years ago, is one of the best preserved in Anuradhapura.

©Charles Walker Collection/Stock Montage, Inc.

Even in translation, the chronicles were difficult to use as historical sources. The *Mahavamsa* was written hundreds of years after some of the events it describes. Alongside passages that seemed factual—the name of a king or the location of his court—were such obviously unfactual accounts as the story of a person zooming through the air. The *Mahavamsa* and other chronicles sometimes contradicted one another, with different accounts of Vijaya and his origins, for example. The biggest problem was that the chronicles were written mainly to glorify Buddhism in Sri Lanka, not to record objectively what happened.

The greatest importance of the *Mahavamsa* is not as history but as a symbol—and as a motivating force behind Sinhalese nationalism. A Sinhalese politician speaking in public is likely to mention incidents from the *Mahavamsa* as evidence of the long and distinguished history the Sinhalese have in Sri Lanka. But Sinhalese political and religious leaders also use *Mahavamsa* stories as evidence that the whole island should be ruled by Sinhalese Buddhists.

of one royal dynasty (ruling family) and supporters of another or between one clan and another.

Anuradhapura remained the strongest kingdom on the island from about 200 B.C. until just before A.D. 1000. During the last 500 years or so of this period, Anuradhapura had control over the other kingdoms to the south. From time to time, the dynasty ruling Anuradhapura would change. A king might die with no obvious successor, for example, and someone from a different family might claim the throne.

On a few occasions, control of Anuradhapura passed to rulers who invaded from southern India. Two of these periods are especially important because of their significance to modern Sri Lankans. The first instance was in the second century B.C., when Prince Elara from southern India assumed the throne. A Buddhist king named Duttugamunu, from the southern Sri Lankan kingdom of Rohana, captured the throne from Elara a few decades later. Duttugamunu then

brought most of the island under the control of the kingdom of Anuradhapura.

In modern times, Sinhalese nationalists often mention Duttugamunu's victory over Elara as a symbol of the Sinhalese struggle against supposed Tamil invaders. Historians point out, however, that the ancient combatants probably saw their fight more as a power struggle between two leaders and not as a Sinhalese-Tamil conflict. Elara most likely had supporters who would fit modern definitions of Sinhalese, and Duttugamunu probably had Tamil followers.

The second important invasion from southern India occurred in A.D. 973, when the army of a strong southern Indian empire named Chola invaded Sri Lanka and, over the following 25 years, conquered all of the territory ruled by Anuradhapura. The Chola forces used tiger symbols on their flags and equipment, so the use of the same symbol by the modern Tamil Tigers reminds some Sinhalese of this invasion from southern India more than 1,000 years ago.

Chola rulers moved the capital of the island's main

CHAPTER 2   *The Conflict's Roots*

kingdom southeast to a city called Polonnaruwa. The capital remained there even after Sinhalese forces defeated the Cholas in 1070. The kingdom, once again under Buddhist leaders, maintained control of most of the island until about 1200. Then weak kings and constant battles for the throne led to the gradual breakup of the kingdom. After this, various cities— mostly in the southwestern quarter of the island— became capitals for less-powerful kings, whose rule usually extended to some of the surrounding countryside but not much farther. The most important of these Buddhist capitals was Kotte, southeast of Colombo.

While the Buddhist kingdom was splintering, Jaffna-patnam, a kingdom ruled by Tamils, was strengthening in the north. This kingdom had its capital near Jaffna, and in the 1300s the realm expanded southward to areas across the Jaffna Lagoon. By this time, the area around Anuradhapura and Polonnaruwa had been almost deserted by the Sinhalese. The Tamil and the Sinhalese kingdoms ruled different parts of

The architectural development that began in Anuradhapura was continued in Polonnaruwa. This structure—the Vatadage (Watadage)—was built as a relic house, in which Buddhist leaders kept a relic of the Buddha.

the island, with a largely un-inhabited, malaria-infested area in between. Tamils controlled the north from their capital at Jaffna, while Sinhalese rulers held sway over the region surrounding Kotte and over the south-central Kandyan region.

But the Tamils and the Sinhalese of the island still had lots of contact with one another. There were Tamil speakers in the Sinhalese areas and Sinhala speakers in the Tamil areas. The Buddhist and Hindu religions continued to influence each other, as did the Sinhala and Tamil languages.

By the 1400s, ethnic consciousness may have gained importance in Sri Lanka. People probably began to think of themselves as either Sinhalese or Tamil in addition to associating with a certain religion, caste, family, and tribe.

Ever since Buddhism disappeared from India in the fifth and sixth centuries, Buddhists in Sri Lanka had been determined to make the island a Buddhist haven. Buddhist monks wrote accounts that spoke ill of non-Buddhists, particularly Tamils. But how far such ethnic feelings or religious identities spread through the general population is an unanswered question. In any case, this ethnic consciousness, if it existed, was certainly far weaker in fifteenth-century Sri Lanka than it has proved to be in modern times.

Caste is an important tool of social organization in Sri Lanka. Each person is born into a particular caste that defines the individual's place within society. The castes—traditionally based on family occupations—form a hierarchy. To retain their purity, those in higher castes avoid close contact with those in lower castes.

Both the Sinhalese and the Tamils adhere to caste systems, although the two systems are distinct from one another. Among the Tamils, the caste system is closely linked to the Hindu religion. Derived from the Brahman-dominated caste system of southern India, the Sri Lankan Tamil caste system respects purity and discriminates against low castes, such as those to which the Indian Tamils belong. The Vellala are the dominant caste among Sri Lankan Tamils, comprising more than half the population. The Vellala formed the elite in the ancient Jaffna kingdom and also maintained large land holdings.

Among the Sinhalese, members of the Goyigama caste make up about half the population. Traditionally, Goyigama filled the royal courts and owned much of the farming land. Goyigama still dominate Sri Lankan politics, and most wealthy landlords are Goyigama. Members of the Karava, Durava, and Salagama castes rate slightly lower than Goyigama. Caste structures in the high country differ from those of the Lowland Sinhalese, typically adhering to more rigid standards in the high country.

For both the Tamils and the Sinhalese, caste fades in importance in urban settings, being applied almost exclusively to marriage arrangements. For example, a Goyigama may not marry a member of a lower caste but wouldn't worry about eating with that person or sitting next to him or her on a bus.

EUROPEANS ARRIVE

Sri Lanka had long been a trading stop for sailors from many lands. Spices, especially cinnamon and pepper, were valuable commodities that attracted Arab sailors, from whom some of the modern Muslims in Sri Lanka are descended. In the 1500s, though, a new type of visitor began arriving at Sri Lanka's shores—Europeans with well-armed gunships and the desire to build a global trade system. First came the Portuguese, then the Dutch, and later the British.

The Portuguese, who had already established colonies in India, first visited Sri

Lanka in 1505, when ships heading for India were blown off course. By making trade deals with the rulers of Sri Lanka's kingdoms, the Portuguese eventually took control of most of the important ports on the island and set up their own administration. By 1619, Portuguese colonizers had control over almost all of Sri Lanka, including Jaffna. The only part of the island that the Portuguese never conquered was the kingdom of Kandy in the south-central highlands. The Portuguese brought the Roman Catholic religion to the island, and the large number of Sri Lankan Roman Catholics with Portuguese names remains as part of Portugal's legacy.

Portugal and the Netherlands were long-standing rivals for trade and land along the rim of the Indian Ocean. Portugal's strength deteriorated when the country fell under Spanish rule in the late 1500s and early 1600s. The Dutch, eager to challenge Portugal's hold on Sri Lanka, got their chance by making an alliance with the king of Kandy in 1638. The following year, the Dutch took over the eastern port of Trincomalee. They eventually captured Portuguese holdings such as Negombo in the west, Galle in the south, and—in 1656—Colombo.

Once they had overcome the Portuguese at Colombo, the Dutch disregarded the help they had received from the Kandyans and refused to share power with them. The king of Kandy retreated to the mountains and concentrated on keeping the Dutch out of his highland kingdom. The Dutch went on to seize the northern ports of Mannar and Jaffna and finally ended Portuguese control in Sri Lanka in 1658.

The Dutch ruled much of Sri Lanka for about 140 years. Their power was strongest along the coasts, where they set up centers of administration in Colombo, Galle, and Jaffna. Their main interest was to trade in Sri Lanka's exotic products, such as cinnamon and elephants, but they also tried to impose some aspects of Dutch culture on Sri Lanka. For example, the Dutch brand of Christianity—Calvinist Protestantism—was promoted by Dutch administrators who tried, unsuccessfully, to eliminate Roman Catholicism on the island.

THE BRITISH PERIOD

Events in Europe eventually brought an end to the Dutch era in Sri Lanka. In 1796, after French armies captured the Netherlands, British forces based in India rushed to take over Sri Lanka before the French could seize the island. Britain, which was already a strong power in India, treated Sri Lanka as part of its Indian Empire. In 1802 the island was declared a separate British colony, called Ceylon.

Unlike the Portuguese and the Dutch, the British were able to conquer Kandy, bringing the entire island under their rule in 1815. Kandy was a Buddhist kingdom that, according to Sinhalese-Buddhist tradition, had preserved the rule established thousands of years earlier by Vijaya. As a result, the kingdom has held a special place in the Sinhalese tradition—even though the last kings of Kandy were not Sinhalese but Tamil. What mattered most to the Kandyans was not so much whether their kings were ethnically Sinhalese as whether they supported Buddhism.

The British had maneuvered their way into the

When Britain took over the island of Sri Lanka, about 800,000 people lived there. The Sinhalese, numbering about 400,000, populated mainly the southwestern coast. Tamils, who lived mainly in the north and east, numbered about 200,000. The Kandyans of the central highlands numbered about 200,000 as well.

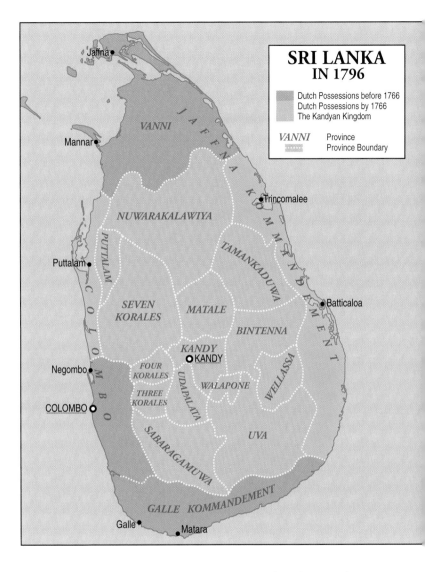

SRI LANKA
IN 1796

Dutch Possessions before 1766
Dutch Possessions by 1766
The Kandyan Kingdom

VANNI   Province
·········· Province Boundary

Kandyan kingdom by exploiting rivalries among Kandyans and by using military force to back their favorite Kandyan leaders. After gaining control, the British appeared to the Kandyans to be protectors of Buddhism. But when the British refused to allow the Kandyans to appoint a new king in 1817, a serious rebellion arose, spread widely, and was crushed brutally the next year. British rule over the entire island survived, but the British were seen by many Sri Lankans—most importantly by the Buddhist monks—as overlords not to be trusted.

The Relic of the Tooth

Near the highland city of Kandy, in one of the holiest temples in Sri Lanka, sits an ornate casket containing a small, whitish object, unquestionably a tooth. Whose? Most Sinhalese Buddhists believe it is a tooth from Buddha, an Indian philosopher who died in 483 B.C.

Legend says that as Hindu rulers in India were persecuting Buddhists about 1,600 years ago, a devout Buddhist princess hid the sacred tooth in her hair and smuggled it to safety in Sri Lanka. The Buddhist kings of early Sri Lanka guarded the tooth as part of their royal obligation to protect Buddhism. A strong connection then grew between the tooth and the island's royalty. No leader could be considered truly legitimate by devout Buddhists unless that ruler protected the tooth.

This remained true even when the guardians of the tooth were not Sinhalese Buddhists. The last kings of Kandy, who were Tamils, also guarded the tooth and kept up the royal tradition of defending Buddhism. Meanwhile, as British powers in coastal Sri Lanka seemed ready to advance against Kandy, the monks who tended the tooth slipped away into the jungle and hid it.

In 1815 John D'Orly, the first British resident (protector of British interests) in the newly conquered Kandyan kingdom,

Embassy of Sri Lanka

greatly impressed the monks. D'Orly had learned to speak Sinhalese, and he took seriously British promises to protect Buddhism and to respect its customs. The monks believed they could trust D'Orly, so they brought the sacred tooth out of its jungle hiding place and put it back in the Temple of the Tooth. This was a symbol that D'Orly could legitimately rule—as long as he continued to safeguard Buddhism.

A couple of years later, during the Great Rebellion of 1818, a man claiming to be related to the royal family of Kandy attempted to chase the British out. By this time, the Kandyans had realized that very few British administrators shared D'Orly's positive attitude toward Buddhism, so the monks decided to support the rebellion. The tooth was again removed from the temple and hidden away, and for a while it looked as if the rebellion might succeed—as if the British, deprived of the tooth, would be driven out.

Some time later, a group of British patrols in Kandy's backcountry got a lucky break— they stumbled upon the hiding place of the tooth. They took the sacred prize and marched back into Kandy. Despair fell upon the Buddhists, who had hoped to be free of British control. They feared the foreigners' luck in finding the tooth must be a sign that they should rule Sri Lanka. Soon after, the rebellion failed.

The British, like the Dutch and Portuguese before them, were chiefly interested in exploiting Sri Lanka's cinnamon, peppers, and other products, most of which were collected from the forests or raised by local farmers on small plots. The British established a different kind of farm in Ceylon—the plantation, or, in British English, estate. Estates covered large areas of land and were devoted entirely to one crop, which was sold and shipped far away.

Coffee was the first estate crop tried by the British in Ceylon. The bean grew well in the highlands for a while, but a disease wiped out the coffee bushes in the late 1800s. After that, the British introduced tea to the highlands and rubber to the lower slopes. Both have thrived for more than a century.

Tea leaves and latex (liquid from a rubber tree used to make rubber) cannot be efficiently harvested by machine. Instead, people must walk slowly among tea bushes, often over steep terrain, to pluck ripe tea leaves. To gather latex, someone must carefully cut a groove in the bark of each rubber tree

This engraving shows workers tapping rubber trees.

to channel the milky substance into a cup. Because harvesting was so much work, the managers of Ceylon's new tea and rubber estates needed far more laborers than they could find on the island. The British planters looked to India—in particular to Tamil-speaking areas of southern India—for estate workers.

The demand for labor resulted in a large movement of Tamil-speaking Indians to the Sri Lankan highlands and to some estates on lower ground. The newcomers shared a language and a religion with most of the Tamils whose ancestors had settled in Sri Lanka many centuries earlier. Still, these Estate Tamils, or Indian Tamils—who mainly came from low-caste backgrounds and had little education—did not mix much with the Ceylon Tamils. The foreigners earned very little money and were housed in barracks. Long-established Ceylon Tamil families, some of whom were wealthy and working in highly skilled professions, felt they had little in common with these newcomers. Ethnic similarities meant less to the Ceylon Tamils than did economic or social differences.

Like many Europeans of the late 1800s and early 1900s, British colonial administrators were deeply interested in race, the term they used to mean approximately what people now call

A British print advertisement from 1897 touts Ceylon-grown tea.

CHAPTER 2 *The Conflict's Roots*

ethnicity. The British tried to analyze and classify the many peoples they encountered in their colonies, in part to figure out which were most "advanced" (that is, most like the British).

But British researchers were not just trying to make themselves feel superior. Most were sincerely interested in understanding the cultures of the people they ruled and in learning their languages. Ultimately, British administrators hoped to use such knowledge to quell disturbances in the colonies and to rule in a way that created as little unrest as possible—without ever giving up their own dominance.

The British tried to accommodate the various "races" they saw within Ceylon. Laws regarding marriage and other customs should be different, they thought, for each group. Representitives from each ethnic group worked on councils that advised the British administration. In each village, the language spoken by the majority would be the one used for official business.

These principles, however noble, led to an almost comical rise in the number of cat-egories among the people of this small island. At one point, there were different family-law codes for two kinds of Tamils (Ceylon Tamils and Indian Tamils), two kinds of Sinhalese (highland and low-country), two kinds of Muslims (coastal and inland), and several kinds of mixed-race Eurasians.

People who had previously considered their Sinhala-ness or Tamil-ness as only a part of their identity—less important than being from a certain village, or family, or caste—were now forced to think of ethnicity as perhaps the most important aspect. After all, before you could figure out which family law applied to you or who represented you on a government council, you had to slot yourself into an ethnic group. In Sri Lanka, this was not always easy. This system of categories was later simplified, but its effects on Sri Lankans'

sense of identity did not go away.

British administration in Ceylon lasted until 1947—about as long as Dutch rule had endured. But the British left a much deeper mark on the island than did the Dutch. For one thing, the English language and the An-glican religion spread among Sri Lankans much farther than did Dutch or Calvinism. For another, British administrators inadvertently organized Sri Lankan society in a way that promoted ethnic divisions.

RELIGIOUS REVIVALS

Religious revivals in both Hinduism and Buddhism during the British period became another factor in the divisions taking place among Sri Lankans. A rekindling of Hindu beliefs spread from southern India to Sri Lanka in the early 1800s. This movement encouraged Sri

> *People who had previously considered their Sinhala-ness or Tamil-ness as only a part of their identity—less important than being from a certain village, or family, or caste—were now forced to think of ethnicity as perhaps the most important aspect.*

Lankan Hindus to take more interest in their own religion and culture and, in particular, to set up a Hindu school system that might rival in quality the island's British-run Christian schools. For a time, Jaffna was the world's greatest center of Tamil Hindu literature and scholarship.

A Buddhist revival in Ceylon in the mid-1800s became even more significant in Sri Lankan history. The renewed growth of Buddhism stressed the importance of schools that compete with the Christian schools, but the movement was tinged with a lot of negative feeling toward non-Buddhists.

One belief many Buddhists shared was a fear that the revitalized Hinduism on the island might overwhelm Sri Lankan Buddhism. The British practice of importing mostly Hindu plantation workers from India compounded Buddhist fears of becoming outnumbered.

An elaborate Hindu temple—called a kovil in Sri Lanka—adorns a streetcorner in Kandy.

Sinhalese preachers unsettled their audiences by pointing out that a huge subcontinent with a hundred million Hindus lay just to the northwest. The idea of Sri Lanka as a Buddhist fortress in a Hindu sea became increasingly popular.

The renewed belief that Sri Lanka had a special Buddhist destiny was encouraged by early Buddhist chronicles such as the *Mahavamsa*. In the middle and late nineteenth century, these writings—previously read mostly by monks and theologians—became much more widely known. The *Mahavamsa*'s legends about the island's ancient heroes and kings reinforced a feeling among the Sinhalese that to be truly Sri Lankan was to be Sinhalese and that to be truly Sinhalese was to be Buddhist. Many Sinhalese Buddhists felt that other citizens—Tamils, Muslims, and even Sinhalese Christians—could never be fully Sri Lankan. This belief came to be known as Sinhalese **nationalism.**

One of the most outspoken and influential Sinhalese nationalists at the turn of the century was Anagarika

Dharmapala, a very prominent Sri Lankan lecturer and writer. Dharmapala started out as a follower of a couple of colorful characters in the Buddhist revival, Colonel Henry Steel Olcott and Madame Helena Petrovna Blavatsky.

Colonel Olcott was a showy American who spearheaded a movement to merge all the world's religions. He came with the Russian-born Madame Blavatsky to Ceylon in 1880 to help local Buddhists debate against Christian missionaries. Dharmapala admired Olcott's pro-Buddhist activities and eventually took them many steps further.

Perhaps more than any other person, Dharmapala was responsible for popularizing the faulty impression that Tamils and Sinhalese had been deadly enemies in Sri Lanka for nearly 2,000 years. He often quoted the *Mahavamsa* as if it were a completely factual account, and his favorite passages were those that made the Tamils sound like pagan invaders who were ruining the island. Much of his preaching and writing was very racist. Dharmapala insisted that the Sinhalese were racially pure Aryans—by which he meant that they had racial ties with north Indians, Iranians, and Europeans. He contrasted the Sinhalese racial line with that of the Dravidian Tamils, which he claimed was inferior.

Even though Dharmapala's lectures and writings were quite popular among the Sinhalese, his message did not at that time inspire ethnic violence. What unrest there was in the late nineteenth and early twentieth centuries was usually religious. In 1883 riots erupted in the Colombo suburb of Kotahena when Sinhalese Roman Catholics tried to break up a Sinhalese Buddhist procession going past St. Lucia's Cathedral. Buddhists and Muslims were at each others' throats several times, notably in 1915 and 1918. Hindus and Muslims, too, clashed occasionally.

DRIVE FOR INDEPENDENCE

Another trend in Sri Lanka, somewhat inspired by Dharmapala, was a lot of anti-British feeling. Dharmapala railed against the Europeans as filthy, drunken, and decadent (even as he went out of his way to prove racial connections between the Sinhalese and the Europeans). Relations between Sinhalese Buddhists and the British reached an especially low point after the 1915 Buddhist-Muslim riots, when the British blamed Buddhists for most of the violence and punished some of their leaders quite severely.

Most anti-British activity in Ceylon however, was peaceful and within the bounds of the law. Many Sri Lankans joined a growing independence movement led mainly by English-speaking professionals, many of whom were graduates of the best schools in Ceylon and Britain. These leaders were inspired in their activities by the nonviolent Indian independence movement going on at the same time. The members of this "English-speaking elite"—Sinhalese, Tamils, and Muslims alike—lived very differently from the mass of poorer Sri Lankans. But their popular support came from being successful locals and not foreigners.

The British, too, got along reasonably well with the

members of this elite group and admired and encouraged the prestigious educational backgrounds and European habits of these Sri Lankans. In an experiment unique among British colonies, adult Sri Lankans (both male and female, of all ethnic groups) had been voting since as early as the 1930s. They elected representatives to a council that, while not really making the colony's laws, did advise the British governor. This experience gave the members of the local political elite, who formed the council, some practice governing according to a British model.

By the time World War II began in 1939, the British had neither the money nor the strength to hold their empire together. The best they could hope for in Ceylon and their other colonies was a peaceful transfer of power to native leaders who might allow British companies to keep operating and who might preserve some British influence. Because of the existence of an English-speaking elite, the British could more easily imagine this happening in Ceylon than in other parts of their empire and felt that if any colony could rule itself in a manner acceptable to British tastes, Ceylon could.

In December 1947, after years of negotiation between the British and some of Ceylon's English-educated elite, King George VI of Britain approved Ceylon's independence. On February 4, 1948—after more than 400 years under European control—the island returned to rule by its own people.

Sri Lanka was soon to face the question that has troubled it ever since: Is it one nation or two? ⊕

By the 1930s, the bustling capital of Colombo had taken on a lot of British characteristics. Shop names and traffic signs were written in English, while imported British autos and clothing styles were common sights on the street.

3

THE PRESENT CONFLICT

The new nation got off to a peaceful start. The first prime minister of independent Ceylon was Don Stephen Senanayake. Senanayake was Sinhalese, but his political party, the United National Party (UNP), included some Tamils as well. Although minorities had little power in the new legislature, most Sinhalese lawmakers seemed willing to work with them and to consider their needs.

TROUBLE FOR MINORITIES

The biggest exception to minority involvement concerned the Estate Tamils. They suffered a great setback in 1948 and 1949, when the national legislature passed laws declaring most of them noncitizens. This change meant that the majority of Indian Tamils lost the right to vote. Those who had official documents proving their ancestry and detailing their travels could apply for Sri Lankan citizenship. Very few laborers in company barracks had any such papers. Almost a million of these Indian Tamils did not qualify for Indian citizenship either and found themselves with no country to call their own.

Other seeds of trouble quietly grew during the country's first eight years of self-rule. Before indepen-

On February 4, 1948, Britain formally granted independence to Ceylon. Don Stephen Senanayake, a leader in the independence movement, became the new nation's first prime minister. In this photo taken just before the independence ceremony, Senanayake appears (fifth from the left) with British officials, Sri Lankan leaders, and other heads of state.

dence a feeling of Sri Lankan nationalism—the desire to expel the British and to create an independent nation—had encouraged Tamil, Sinhalese, and Muslim leaders to work together. After independence this feeling faded. Replacing it was an increased **communalism,** a focus on the interests of one's own ethnic or religious group rather than on the interests of Sri Lankan society as a whole.

Even the Sinhalese felt disadvantaged, despite being the majority. There was a common feeling among the Sinhalese that before independence the British had favored the Tamils for government jobs. Whether this was true or not, most Sinhalese believed it. By stereotyping the Tamils as selfish, English-speaking parasites living off the system handed down by the British, Sinhalese extremists stirred up a lot of anti-Tamil feeling—with the language issue at its heart. The Sinhalese nationalist claim that Sri Lanka should be a Sinhala-speaking, Buddhist nation increased in popularity.

As Sinhalese nationalism grew, so did uneasiness among the minorities, particularly the Tamils. They felt anything but privileged. Government programs had begun in the 1930s to relocate poor Sinhalese families to parts of the north and east—territories the Tamils considered part of their traditional homeland. Already a minority in the new

A Land of Many Names

It was only in 1972 that Sri Lanka officially became Sri Lanka. From the British colonial era to the early 1970s, the island was officially known as Ceylon. Some older Tamils still prefer to call the country Ceylon because they prefer the British term to the current Sinhalese name. It's likely, though, that Ceylon is simply a variant of Sri Lanka—based on a British misunderstanding of what islanders were saying when they were asked the name of the place.

In Sinhala-language texts, the island has long been referred to as Lanka. The *Sri* added to the front is an honorific, a small word whose only function is to add a tone of greatness to the name. Early Buddhist chronicles in the Pali language referred to the island as *Sihaladipa,* a name in which the first part *(Sihala)* means "lion" and the second *(dipa)* means "island." This name reflects a traditional story that the Sinhalese are descended from a lion.

Tamil separatists often speak of breaking away to form a new nation called Eelam. This word is derived from *Ila,* a traditional Tamil-language name for the entire island. Evidence suggests that this Tamil name may have been derived from the Pali word *Sihala.*

The island had one other interesting name, also derived from the word *Sihaladipa.* To the Arab traders who visited Sri Lanka long ago, the island was known as *Serendib* or, in English, Serendip. The name comes from a Persian fairy tale called "The Three Princes of Serendip," in which the princes—who came from Lanka—set off on adventures and, while they were looking for one thing, would stumble upon something better.

From this, the English language gets the word *serendipity,* which means the habit or process of unexpectedly making a great discovery while trying to find something else.

nation, the Tamils feared becoming a minority in their home regions. They also knew that government plans were under way to make it harder for speakers of Tamil to get into the best schools.

Trouble for most non-Sinhalese came in 1956, a year that was being celebrated as the 2,500th anniversary of the Buddha's death. Dharmapala's writings remained popular, and Sinhalese-Buddhist nationalism was running high. A nationwide election had been rescheduled to be held that year, and the leaders of the Sri Lanka Freedom Party (SLFP) tried to attract the votes of the Sinhalese majority with pro-Sinhalese campaign promises. Most importantly, they vowed to make Sinhala the only official language of the island.

After the SLFP secured a majority in parliament, its leader, Solomon West Ridgeway Dias (SWRD) Bandaranaike, became prime minister. Soon a law called the Official Language Act No. 33 of 1956—often known as the Sinhala-Only Act—was ap-

SWRD Bandaranaike addresses a crowd at a rally in 1955. Bandaranaike and the SLFP captured control of the government with a pro-Sinhalese campaign.

UPI/Bettmann

Speaking English in Sri Lanka

One major language of Sri Lanka not strongly associated with any one ethnic group is English. The English language is widely used in business, in the press, and sometimes in government. Before Ceylon's independence from Britain in 1948—and even for a few years afterwards—fluency in English was essential to a career in government, law, or medicine. Many older Sri Lankans went to schools where all lessons were taught in English.

Shortly after independence, Sri Lankans were eager to switch from English to their native languages in the business environment. The move toward *swibasha*—local languages—in official dealings made sense for every community in the nation. But when English was eventually unseated as the language of government, Sri Lanka embarked on a rocky road. The Official Language Act No. 33 of 1956 said that only Sinhala would be an official language. Sri Lanka's minorities—with the exception of the very few who could speak Sinhala—were put at a disadvantage. Not until 1988 did a constitutional amendment make Sinhala and Tamil equal as joint official languages.

Although it is no longer an official language, English remains important in Sri Lanka, and visitors can usually find someone with whom to communicate in English. Not only is English internationally useful but it also gives Sri Lankans of different native languages a second language—albeit a foreign language—in which to communicate.

---

proved by the legislature.

This law was originally written to allow the "reasonable" use of Tamil in some government transactions. But Sinhalese extremists, including powerful Buddhist monks (called *bhikkus*), objected. The government couldn't afford to lose the support of the powerful monks, so the eventual law was firm and extreme—no Tamil, no English, nothing but Sinhala would be allowed in any dealings between Sri Lankans and their government. The non-Sinhalese of the island would have to either learn Sinhala or hire a translator every time they needed to fill out a government form or write to a government office.

Beyond the great inconveniences it created, the law insulted the Tamils and other minorities by treating them as outsiders in their own land. Predictably, protests followed. Some Tamils demonstrating in Colombo were beaten up by Sinhalese extremists and rural Sinhalese killed more than a hundred Tamils near Amparai, one of the colonization sites in the eastern part of the island.

From then on, relations between the Sinhalese and the minorities only got worse. Seemingly trivial events touched off explosions of emotion. For example, many Tamils were outraged over a government ruling that the license plates of all Sri Lankan vehicles had to bear the Sinhala character *sri*, meaning "great" or "wonderful." (A character is a basic unit of writing, like a letter of the alphabet.)

EARLY ETHNIC RIOTS

The protests eventually had an impact. In 1957 Bandaranaike promised to allow some use of Tamil in official business and to give local

Tamil satyagrahis, *or peaceful demonstrators, sat outside government offices in Jaffna in 1961, protesting the Sinhala-Only Act.*

councils more influence in the day-to-day government of Tamil areas. Then, under pressure from Buddhist monks and other Sinhalese groups, he backed out of the deal. Tamil leaders planned a nonviolent protest (called a *satyagraha*) in May 1958, but Sinhalese activists attacked buses carrying Tamils to the protest site. Word of the attack spread quickly and emboldened Sinhalese mobs throughout the island, including in Colombo, to attack Tamils and Tamil-owned property in Sinhalese-dominated areas. At least 100 people, mostly Tamils, were killed, and many hundreds of others were injured. About 12,000 Tamils in western and central Sri Lanka lost their homes and fled to the northeast or to India.

Throughout the 1960s and 1970s, the Sinhalese-dominated government continued to favor the Sinhalese and to make life difficult for the minorities. Although a law enacted in 1966 allowed some use of Tamil for official business in the north and east, Sinhala remained the country's only official language. New rules for university admission required higher test scores from Tamil-speaking applicants than from Sinhala-speaking ones. And when the country's constitution was changed in 1972, Buddhism was honored as the foremost religion in the country. Among the Tamils, separatism—the desire to form a separate Tamil state—became more popular.

The largest Tamil political party changed its name in 1976 to the Tamil United Liberation Front (TULF) and called for the Northern and Eastern Provinces to break away peacefully from Sri Lanka and form a separate Tamil state. Because several TULF members represented the northern and eastern districts in the national legislature, Sri Lanka's government was in the unusual position of having legislators who advocated the breakup of the country.

But when another major conflict erupted in Sri Lanka, it did not rise from Tamil separatism. In 1971 serious rioting began in Colombo and in other places around the island. Behind the riots was the JVP, a radi-

In 1959 a Buddhist monk assassinated SWRD Bandaranaike. The monk, a Sinhalese extremist, was only one of many Sinhalese displeased with Bandaranaike's concessions to Sri Lankan Tamils. After the assassination, Sirimavo Bandaranaike, the slain leader's wife, took office as the world's first female prime minister. She served as the nation's leader until 1965 and again from 1970 to 1977. In 1994 she was again appointed prime minister, under the regime led by her daughter, President Chandrika Kumaratunga.

Sirimavo Bandaranaike

cal group of mostly young and poor Sinhalese who aimed to overthrow the Sri Lankan government because they felt it was doing too little to improve life for the Sinhalese.

The government responded harshly, outlawing the JVP and using great force to hunt down and kill suspected JVP members. The Sri Lankan government also declared a state of emergency that lasted until early 1977—long after this JVP revolt had been crushed. Throughout the 1970s, the government used its emergency powers to limit the activities of dissident groups—particularly Tamil separatists, who had nothing to do with the 1971 uprising.

THE JAYEWARDENE YEARS

Big political changes came to Sri Lanka in the late 1970s, when the United National Party unseated the SLFP in the country's legislature. For all but five of the years from 1960 to 1977, the SLFP's Sirimavo Bandaranaike had led Sri Lanka's government. When her party was crushingly defeated in the 1977 parliamentary elections, Junius Richard Jayewardene, the leader of the UNP, became prime minister with more than 80 percent of the seats in parliament—an almost unheard-of majority in parliament.

With such a majority, the UNP could pass almost any law it liked. Jayewardene in-

Students from the University of Ceylon in Colombo marched out of the Parliament building after holding a demonstration in the lobby in 1969. Tension grew between the government and Sinhalese student groups in the late 1960s and early 1970s, as Sinhalese students pushed for a reduction in the number of Tamil students allowed to enroll in the university.

Archive Photos/AFP

troduced a new constitution in 1978 that made the prime minister's office much less powerful but greatly increased the authority of the president. He himself became the first president of Sri Lanka under this new system, which is still in place.

At first it seemed as if the new UNP government might make progress toward solving the country's worsening ethnic divisions. The UNP's official statements in 1977 admitted that the Tamils faced unjust discrimination. The 1978 constitution recognized Tamil and Sinhala as national languages, even though Sinhala remained the only official language. Jayewardene even supported a system of district councils—local governing bodies that could give the Tamils a greater voice in administering northern and eastern regions.

But the Jayewardene government made other changes as well. One was a new law called the Prevention of Terrorism Act. Passed in 1979, this act gave the police extremely broad powers to arrest suspects, deny them any contact with the outside world, and keep them locked away without a trial.

> *Jayewardene made clear that this long-lived government would take special care of Sinhalese Buddhists.*

With his party's huge majority in parliament, Jayewardene was able to arrange for elections and constitutional amendments that assured him and his party of staying in power until at least 1989 if they wanted to. He made clear that this long-lived government would take special care of Sinhalese Buddhists. He arranged to have the *Mahavamsa* updated, a gesture that recalled Sri Lanka's ancient kings and their guardianship of Buddhism. He even asked the people to address him as *devi yanse* (Your Excellency), a term intended to associate him with the kings of precolonial Sri Lanka.

Meanwhile, various Tamil separatist groups were forming in Sri Lanka and among Sri Lankan Tamils in other countries. Many of the organizations were willing to use violence to promote their aims. The best-known of these militant separatist groups, the Liberation Tigers of Tamil Eelam, took shape in 1972 (until 1978 they were known as the Tamil New Tigers). In 1978 the Tamil Tigers blew up an Air Lanka commercial airliner on the ground in Colombo. They also eventually claimed responsibility for the first murder attributed to Tamil separatist rebels—the 1975 assassination of the mayor of Jaffna, a Tamil whose support for the Sri Lankan government angered the rebels.

Sri Lankan Tamils in other countries began sending money to separatists back home. Some of the money was used to smuggle weapons into Sri Lanka and to send young commandos to training camps in the Middle East, North Africa, and India. As the 1970s drew to a close, more and more young Sri Lankan Tamils—shut out of universities, unable to find meaningful employment, and convinced that Sri Lankan society had no room for them—prepared for war.

At this time, rumors abounded that some Tamil separatist groups in Sri Lanka were talking to Tamil separatists in southern India about creating a Tamil nation on the southern tip of the Indian subcontinent that would include northern and eastern Sri Lanka. Such talks may never have gone very far—if they took place at all—but the mere idea of a powerful Tamil state was enough to strengthen Sinhalese nationalists in their belief that Tamils were the enemy. Anti-Tamil riots erupted in the late 1970s, chasing almost all the Tamils out of such north-central cities as Anuradhapura. Most of them fled toward Jaffna and India.

Ethnic tensions exploded in 1981. As early as April of that year, the police and young Tamils in the north and east were involved in gun battles. Things got much worse in June, during an election campaign in the north.

After two Sinhalese police officers were killed, angry Sinhalese ran through the city of Jaffna, destroying Tamil property and burning the public library, which contained many irreplaceable historical documents in Tamil. Some reports said that the burning of the library was committed not by mobs but by the police themselves. The following months saw even more anti-Tamil violence in several locations throughout the country—near Colombo, in mining towns, in the hill country, and near the east coast. But, as disturbing as the 1981 riots were, worse was yet to come.

FROM BAD TO WORSE

Throughout early 1983—the year often cited as the beginning of true civil war in Sri Lanka—the Tamil separatists and the government exchanged accusations of one offense or another. In various Tamil areas—Jaffna, Mannar, and Vavuniya—emergency regulations restricted the movement of the people. Then, on July 3, the government instituted Emergency Regulation 15A, a new rule that allowed the immediate burial or cremation of anyone the army killed. The soldiers didn't even have to identify the person before disposing of the body. This made it almost impossible to investigate whether a killing was justified. Together with the Prevention of Terrorism Act of 1979, the new law cleared the way for opponents of the government simply to "disappear"—perhaps shot and buried, or thrown in prison with no way of contacting their relatives.

Tamil guerrillas stepped up their terrorism, burning public buses and attacking post offices. Rumors spread that Sinhalese militants were planning to hit the Tamils hard. On July 23, Tamil separatists attacked an army patrol near Jaffna. Thirteen soldiers, all of them Sinhalese, were killed and mutilated.

Instead of being taken to their hometowns for burial, the bodies were flown to Colombo. The memorial cer-

Gangs of Sinhalese youths cruised through Tamil neighborhoods in Colombo destroying as much Tamil property as they could.

A burning body lays in the middle of a street on the outskirts of Colombo on the fifth day of anti-Tamil rioting in July 1983.

emony inflamed anti-Tamil sentiment that had long been smoldering.

Gangs of Sinhalese youths cruised through Tamil neighborhoods in Colombo, destroying as much Tamil property as they could. Tamil residents who resisted were beaten, stabbed, or burned. Some were "necklaced"— burned to death after tires were hung around their necks and set afire. The Tamil neighborhood called Wellawatte was almost totally destroyed by fire.

As the Colombo riots were starting, government security forces near Jaffna dragged 20 Tamils from a train and shot them. President Jayewardene later admitted that these murders occurred, but no soldier ever stood trial for them. In the next few days, 53 Tamil prisoners were killed at Welikade Prison in Colombo.

Although prison authorities blamed other inmates for the deaths, no one was ever tried for them. Since the murdered prisoners had been held in a maximum security wing of the prison—normally beyond the reach of other inmates—prison guards were thought to have cooperated in the murders.

Anti-Tamil violence rolled like a wave throughout the

island, leading to riots in nearly every area where Tamils and Sinhalese lived in close contact. The government declared a curfew throughout the island, making it illegal for anyone but security personnel to be out on the streets, but the security forces hardly enforced it. The violence went on in full force for another two days.

Many eyewitness accounts said that the police and the armed forces—made up almost entirely of Sinhalese—stood by and watched as Tamils were assaulted. Other witnesses accused the security forces and government-sponsored thugs of joining in the destruction. From the very start, the Sinhalese who methodically targeted Tamil properties carried lists so accurate they were thought to be official voter-registration records. Rioters often arrived at the scene in government-owned buses.

To make matters worse, a rumor spread that the Tamil Tigers had invaded Colombo. This false claim led to another widespread slaughter of Tamils. The power of rumor was made greater by the fact that President Jayewar- dene did not address the country about the riots until five days after they had started. In the meantime, Jayewardene holed up in the heavily guarded presidential residence known as Temple Trees and let junior officials do the talking. In the absence of strong and reassuring leadership, the people of Sri Lanka assumed the worst.

When he did speak, on July 28, 1983, Jayewardene had no comfort for the Tamils. He spoke of how much the Sinhalese—and, to a lesser extent, the Muslims—had suffered during the unrest. He said nothing about how bad things had been for the Tamils, the main victims.

During the riots of July 1983, at least 350 and maybe as many as 3,000 Sri Lankans (mostly Tamils) were killed. Between 2,500 and 5,000 businesses were destroyed. At least 150,000 Sri Lankans no longer had jobs because of the destruction. More than 160,000 people became

In 1984 officials found the bodies of 36 victims of LTTE terrorism. The victims had been tied up, shot, and left hidden on a farm in northern Sri Lanka.

UPI/Corbis-Bettmann

homeless refugees. The damage cost Sri Lanka at least $350 million and probably a lot more. All this from about a week of unrest.

As a result of the riots, the divisions in Sri Lankan society deepened. Many moderate Tamils who had once opposed separatism now supported it, after having watched their homes and businesses burn to the ground. Sinhalese Sri Lankans saw the Tamil rebels as the real cause of the riots, and the government encouraged these sentiments.

As fear of the separatist Tamil rebels grew, the government amended the constitution in 1983 to make it a crime to even talk about dividing Sri Lanka. This made the official stand of the leading Tamil party, the TULF, illegal. All 16 TULF members of parliament resigned.

Meanwhile, the government's troops and the Tamil rebels engaged in open war. Much of northern and eastern Sri Lanka—Jaffna, in particular—became a battle zone where rebels launched guerrilla attacks while soldiers patrolled in search of militants. Ordinary people lived in fear of both sides—

A house in Colombo burned during the July 1983 riots.

Drs. A.A.M. van der Heyden, Naerden, the Netherlands

the guerrillas who might attack a bus or a train station at any moment and the government troops who might invade a village and rough up innocent civilians accused of being rebels.

Life in the north became more difficult as the government, trying to cut off supplies to the rebels, blockaded the Jaffna Peninsula. Basic food and medical supplies became scarce for Jaffna's population, which was almost exclusively Tamil.

Dozens of rebel groups fought not only the government but also one another. Although they all wanted Eelam to break away from Sri Lanka, they disagreed about how to do it and about who should be in charge. One group would receive a shipment of arms, and one or two others would stage a raid to capture the valuable hardware. Many of the gun battles between separatist groups occurred in India—especially in the southeast-ern city of Madras—because most of the groups had Indian headquarters and training camps.

By 1986 the Tamil Tigers, led by the intense and self-disciplined Vellupillai Prabhakaran, had wiped out all but four or five rival groups and had become the dominant military force among the separatists. By 1987 the LTTE had about 3,000 armed members and many more unarmed supporters willing to give them food and supplies. With many sympathizers overseas, the Tamil Tigers set up offices in France and Britain and portrayed themselves as a political entity as well as a military force. The more moderate TULF party found itself on the margins of the struggle as the Tigers' radical position appealed to more and more Tamils.

In January 1987, the LTTE declared that they were taking over the administration of the city of Jaffna. The Sri Lankan government responded by blockading Jaffna and sending troops to recapture the city and surrounding

Vellupillai Prabhakaran is said to be clever at disguises. He once slipped away from enemies disguised as a peanut seller and another time dressed as a Roman Catholic priest.

Panos Pictures

Vellupillai Prabhakaran

He is the man the Sri Lankan government most wants to catch—Vellupillai Prabhakaran, the leader of the Liberation Tigers of Tamil Eelam. The government hopes that, like the JVP in 1989, the Tigers might be debilitated by the loss of their leader. But he eluded the Indian army in the late 1980s, when he was their most-wanted target, and he continues to slip through net after net thrown up to catch him.

Born in the town of Vadamarachi on the Jaffna Peninsula, Prabhakaran came from a middle-class family. The political situation into which he was born drew him into the deadly business of militant separatism. Reportedly, he was deeply disturbed by seeing a Hindu holy man burned alive by Sinhalese in the anti-Tamil riots of 1958, when Prabhakaran was only four years old. As an impressionable teenager in the early 1970s, he was surrounded by angry Tamils preaching the separatist cause. Prabhakaran quit high school, formed a group called the Tamil New Tigers in 1972, went to India for training in guerrilla tactics, and learned the terrorist trade. As a young man, Prabhakaran was famous for his good aim with towns from the rebels. A brief truce in April ended after the Tigers shot and killed 126 civilians in the North Central Province. Another militant group, the Eelam Revolutionary Organization of Students, planted a bomb in the main bus station in Colombo. At least 150 people were killed and hundreds of others injured. The government offensive resumed, and soldiers captured several towns on the Jaffna Peninsula. The troops burned down most of Vadamarachi, the hometown of Vellupillai Prabhakaran and other leaders of the Tamil Tigers.

INDIA GETS INVOLVED

At this point, in June 1987, India became fully embroiled in Sri Lanka's problems. In many ways, India had been involved all along. Some Indian Tamils in the highlands and cities of Sri Lanka were citizens of India. In the early 1960s, India had agreed to allow the very gradual immigration of about 500,000 stateless Indian Tamils to India. Waves of Sri Lankan Tamil refugees, about 130,000 people by 1987, came ashore in India each time anti-Tamil violence erupted in Sri Lanka. In addition the southern Indian state of Tamil Nadu had long been almost a second home to many Sri Lankan Tamil separatists. Indian authorities knew that illegal training camps for the Tamil Tigers and other separatist groups were operating on Indian soil.

But one of India's main motives for getting further involved in Sri Lanka was to show itself as the great power of South Asia, responsible for keeping order in the region. If chaos reigned less than 50 miles from India's shores, the nation's credibility as a regional peacekeeper would suffer.

The Indian government had earlier urged the Jayewardene government and the rebels to negotiate a settlement, but that effort failed. In June 1987, India defied the Jayewardene regime and sent boats carrying supplies to Sri Lanka, but the Sri Lankan navy turned them away. The next day, five cargo planes set off, crossed into Sri Lankan airspace without permission,

a rifle and for his brilliance at guerrilla tactics.

Prabhakaran came to public attention in 1975 when the Tamil New Tigers (later known as the Liberation Tigers of Tamil Eelam) assassinated Alfred Duriappah, the Tamil mayor of Jaffna. From among scores of Tamil separatist groups, the Tigers eventually emerged as the most durable and most ruthless, largely because of Prabhakaran's hard-edged leadership and because of their use of small combat groups. The capture of one group does not necessarily lead to information about another. Captured Tigers are not afraid to use the potassium cyanide suicide capsules they carry around their necks—another of Prabhakaran's ideas.

Short and heavily built, with curly black hair, Prabhakaran looks like many another middle-aged Sri Lankan man. But his face is very well known to the Sri Lankan special forces who are eager to capture him. He has eluded them by sleeping in a different house nearly every night, surrounding himself with loyal bodyguards, and disguising himself when in public.

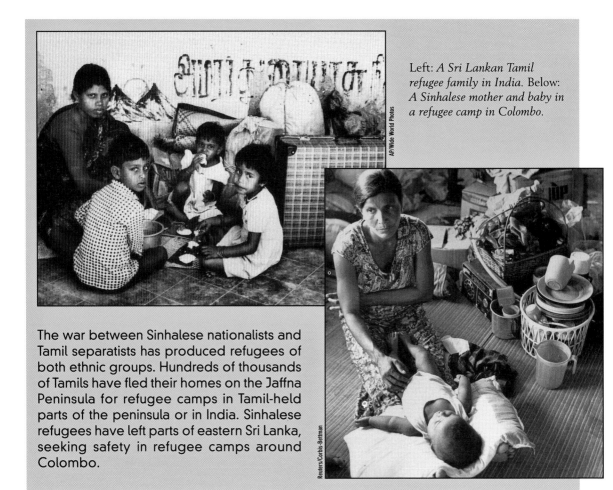

Left: *A Sri Lankan Tamil refugee family in India.* Below: *A Sinhalese mother and baby in a refugee camp in Colombo.*

AP/Wide World Photos

The war between Sinhalese nationalists and Tamil separatists has produced refugees of both ethnic groups. Hundreds of thousands of Tamils have fled their homes on the Jaffna Peninsula for refugee camps in Tamil-held parts of the peninsula or in India. Sinhalese refugees have left parts of eastern Sri Lanka, seeking safety in refugee camps around Colombo.

Reuters/Corbis-Bettman

and landed in Jaffna, breaking the embargo imposed by the Sri Lankan government.

President Jayewardene had no choice but to reach an agreement with his mammoth neighbor to the north. The result was the Indo–Sri Lankan Agreement, signed in Colombo on July 29, 1987,

by President Jayewardene and the Indian prime minister, Rajiv Gandhi. Its provisions to resolve the conflict in Sri Lanka included:

1. The merger of the Northern and Eastern Provinces into one new province, with significant local au-

thority in governing the area.

2. The end of the state of emergency in the north and east.

3. The pardon for any crimes committed by the militants in exchange for the

surrender of the militants' weapons.

4. The return to Sri Lanka of at least 130,000 refugees in camps in India.

5. The recognition of the Tamil and English languages as having equal status with Sinhala as official languages.

6. The possibility of posting Indian soldiers—the Indian Peace-Keeping Force (IPKF)—in Sri Lanka.

Although great hopes were aroused by the agreement, it was in trouble from the start.

Even before it was signed, politicians from parties other than the UNP—including former prime minister Sirimavo Bandaranaike of the SLFP—announced plans to work against it. In the days leading up to Rajiv Gandhi's arrival in Sri Lanka, Colombo was rocked by riots, during which 19 people were killed by the police. A curfew was imposed on the island. While Gandhi was in Colombo for the signing of the pact, police killed five protesters. The day after the signing, one of the Sri Lankan navy honor guards at Gandhi's departure ceremony broke ranks and struck the Indian leader

on the back with his rifle.

After it was signed, the agreement caused even greater trouble—for both India and Sri Lanka. Sinhalese activists, including many Buddhist monks, opposed the pact because they thought it would lead to the founding of a separate Tamil nation. Sinhalese Buddhists, long afraid that Hindu India would chase Buddhism out of Sri Lanka, were furious when Indian troops were eventually sent to the island. Many Tamils rejected the agreement because it stopped short of creating a separate Tamil state. Prabhakaran of the Tamil Tigers,

Buddhist monks in Sri Lanka protest India's June 1987 shipment of food and supplies to Jaffna, a move that broke an embargo imposed on the peninsula by the Sri Lankan government. The embargo, intended to isolate Tamil separatist guerillas, also affected hundreds of thousands of civilians.

Reuters/Arthur Tsang/Archive Photos

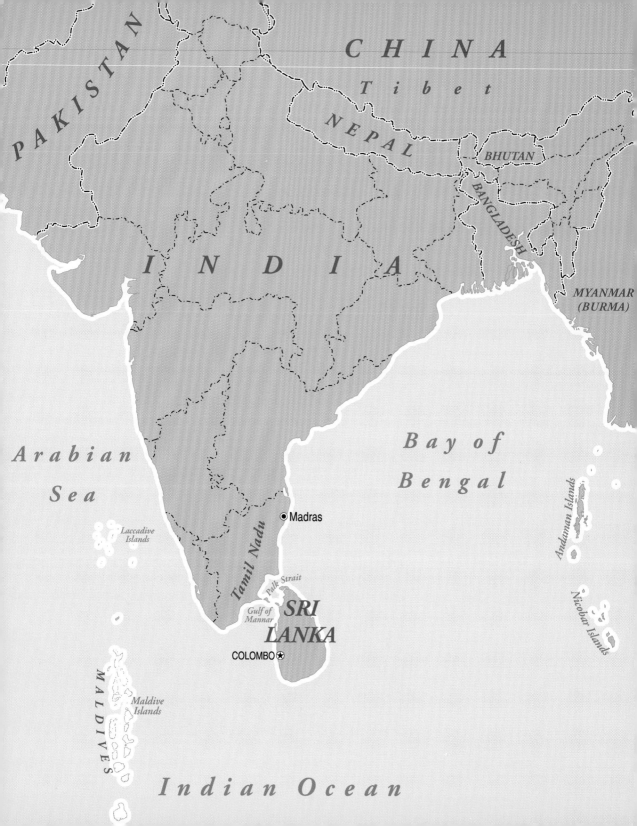

who had been flown to India to preview the pact and had led India to expect his support, spoke out against it less than a week after the signing. Tamil militants made only a weak show of giving up any weapons. Moreover, Sri Lankans of all backgrounds who were still sensitive about foreign colonialism objected to having Indian troops on the island.

It wasn't long before the Indians had a fight on their hands. After Tamil Tigers attacked and murdered five IPKF soldiers on October 8, 1987, the Indians decided to do something the Sri Lankan government had failed to do—root the Tigers out of Jaffna. After almost two weeks of hard fighting, the Indians did manage to capture key parts of the city, but it was not much of a victory. The LTTE agreed to a cease-fire but remained strong and well armed. Many civilians

Sri Lanka's location—next door to India and far from any other country—helps explain why India has had a large influence over affairs on the island of Sri Lanka.

were killed in the fighting, and this badly damaged the Indians' image as peacekeepers. Sinhalese politicians from many parties played on the public's distaste for having foreign soldiers in Sri Lanka. Most significantly, the JVP took advantage of the Indian presence to rise again.

THE JVP RESURFACES

During the late 1980s, the JVP condemned not only the foreign troops in Sri Lanka but also the Jayewardene government that had allowed them in. In a very extreme form, they said what many Sinhalese believed—that the Tamils were being given too many concessions, and the Indian troops were helping the Tamils to get them. In particular, the JVP denounced the creation of both the North-Eastern Province and a system of small district councils to give the Tamils more say in running their own affairs.

The JVP, which previously had been a legal political party, had secretly been building up strength since 1983. By 1987 the JVP had resumed violent activities. That year the JVP launched a

campaign of strikes, bombings, and murders to bring down the Jayewardene government.

On August 18, 1987, a suspected member of the JVP threw a grenade in the Parliament building. The bomb narrowly missed President Jayewardene and Prime Minister Ranasinghe Premadasa, seriously wounded Lalith Athulathmudali, the minister of national security, and killed two other government officials. The murder of cabinet ministers, members of parliament, active members of political parties—even clerks in government offices and candidates in local elections—became a favorite JVP tactic. The organization hoped to shut down the government by intimidating anyone connected with it.

The JVP threat found its way into nearly every aspect of Sri Lankan life. In 1988 all but one university in Sri Lanka closed because of student strikes led by the JVP. When the JVP declared a general strike, ordinary people stayed away from work, not necessarily because they supported the JVP, but because they feared being murdered for disobeying.

Friends and relatives visited the home of Vijaya Kumaratunga in February 1988, a couple of days after the popular actor turned politician was assassinated there. Kumaratunga, who led the SLFP, was to be a candidate in the upcoming presidential election.

Ranasinghe Premadasa, as the UNP candidate. President Jayewardene, 82 years old, had decided not to run again. Premadasa faced Sirimavo Bandaranaike, still the SLFP's leader. Since intimidation of political candidates and voters was one of the JVP's specialties, the upcoming elections provided a fresh field for terrorism.

Sri Lanka seethed with violence—carried out by Tamil guerrillas, JVP assassins, government troops and death squads, and tens of thousands of soldiers from India. At one point in November 1988, increasing violence and a general strike enforced by the JVP crippled Sri Lanka so badly that the fearful government sent home as many foreign tourists and businesspeople as they could find.

Both sets of elections were eventually held, despite an average of six political murders per day in late November 1988. A Muslim party

Shops, schools, public transportation, and basic electricity and water services shut down. Government soldiers had to take over power stations to keep them running.

In late 1988, southern Sri Lanka was in chaos. On September 4, government security forces killed Wijedasa Liyanarachchi, a lawyer who had been arrested in Colombo. He had been representing the families of many JVP members who had "disappeared." Liyanarachchi was found to have been struck at least 100 times with a blunt instrument while in jail. The JVP protested his death by declaring strikes throughout the south.

Another factor stirring up unrest was a pair of important elections—in November for the first governing council of the newly merged North-Eastern Province and in December for president. The JVP bitterly denounced the North-Eastern provincial council as a huge concession to the Tamils.

The presidential vote featured the prime minister,

(the Muslim Congress) and the Eelam People's Revolutionary Liberation Front, an Indian-backed group of Tamil separatists, each took about half of the seats on the North-Eastern provincial council. The Tamil Tigers refused to participate in the elections.

In December Premadasa won the presidency. During the election, he had carefully avoided strong statements against the JVP. After his victory, however, his government cracked down. Operating under emergency regulations, uniformed troops killed or imprisoned almost anyone they wanted to, without facing investigations. On a less official level, but still with the help of Sri Lanka's government, **paramilitary** groups and death squads hunted down suspected JVP guerrillas and executed them on the spot.

The crushing blow to the JVP came in mid-November 1989 when its top two leaders, Rohana Wijeweera and Upatissa Gamanayake, were captured and killed. The government offered explanations for the deaths but cremated the bodies before investigators could confirm the story.

The JVP withered almost immediately in the absence of its top leaders. The group's campaign of slaughter in southern and western Sri Lanka had killed an estimated 25,000 to 60,000 people.

THE TIGERS CLAIM JAFFNA

After two years, the fighting in northern and eastern Sri Lanka continued with little change. In 1989 India began pulling out of the country. The Tamil Tigers—despite having lost hundreds, maybe thousands, of guerrillas in clashes with the Indian

UNP supporters gathered for a final campaign meeting before the December 1988 presidential election, in which UNP candidate Ranasinghe Premadasa (pictured on poster) was victorious.

AP/Wide World Photos

Dinodia Picture Agency

The LTTE has been very successful in recruiting young people—men and women alike—to fight for the Tamil Tiger cause. Many of the recruits have been well-educated but jobless youths with no faith in Sri Lanka's political system. They believe that their only hope for the future lies in the creation of a separate Tamil state.

Reuters/Anuruddha Lokuhapuarachchi/Archive Photos

army—were stronger than ever. They bragged that they had fought the world's fourth-largest army and had won.

Although India's 60,000 troops in northern and eastern Sri Lanka had done little to bring peace, they did help rebuild some of war-ravaged Jaffna. They also assisted in supervising the 1988 elections for the newly created North-Eastern Province. But the cost was high.

Between 1987 and March 24, 1990—when the last Indian soldier left Sri Lanka—1,155 Indian troops had died on the island. About 2,500 others had been wounded. And India had made enemies among both the Tamils and the Sinhalese.

After defeating the JVP, the Sri Lankan government redirected its full attention to the Tamil rebels. As Indian troops departed, the Premadasa government held talks with the LTTE. Having outlasted Indian military efforts to destroy them, the Tigers enjoyed a lot of support from the general Tamil public and were obviously the real power in the north and east. The elected leaders of the North-Eastern provincial council were little more than figureheads, commanding nowhere near the power and support enjoyed by the Tigers. The Sri Lankan government even encouraged Tiger forces to police certain areas as the Indian army vacated them. Officials hoped that the LTTE and other Tamil militants would settle into a peaceful role now that some of their demands—a combined North-Eastern Province, laws to create district councils, and the withdrawal of the Indian army— had been met.

That hope was dashed in June 1990, when LTTE guerrillas attacked several police stations near Batticaloa and Amparai in the east. Hundreds of police officers were captured and many of them killed. Nor was the renewed conflict limited to Sinhalese and Tamils. Massacres of resources and influence, became routine.

The government responded with a big military buildup in an attempt to get rid of the Tigers. When Tiger guerrillas attacked government soldiers in Jaffna's old Dutch fort, government planes bombed the area—still populated by civilians—in a vain effort to break the siege. In the end, the Tigers took the fort, forced the soldiers to flee, and declared themselves the government in Jaffna.

Fierce fighting between the Sri Lankan government and the Tamil Tigers has been the rule since then. At many times, the government has controlled as little as 15 percent of the area of the Jaffna Peninsula—only those areas within the fences of its military bases. Peace talks

---

Having outlasted Indian military efforts to destroy them, the Tigers enjoyed a lot of support from the general Tamil public and were obviously the real power in the north and east.

Muslims by Tamil fighters in the east, where the two groups lived close to one another and competed for between the government and the LTTE have never resulted in much more than a rest period for the Tigers.

ASSASSINATIONS & ELECTIONS

As violence continued into the early 1990s, politicians became popular targets. The Tamil Tigers were suspected of carrying out the suicide bombing in May 1991 that killed India's prime minister, Rajiv Gandhi, while he was visiting the Indian state of Tamil Nadu. The Tigers denied involvement, but India has issued arrest warrants for Prabhakaran and a couple of other Tigers.

In May 1993, President Premadasa was also assassinated, when a bicyclist with a bomb strapped to his body crashed into the president's car, detonating the bomb. Again the Tigers denied responsibility, but they remained the most likely suspects. A UNP politician named Dingiri Banda Wijetunge was appointed to succeed Premadasa.

Parliamentary elections were held in August 1994 and were followed by a presidential election in November. The People's Alliance, a political coalition made up of the SLFP and several other parties, gained a majority in Parliament. This meant that the UNP, the party of Presi-

Military officers guard the casket of President Premadasa, who was assassinated in May 1993. No group took responsibility for the assassination.

too liberal for many Sinhalese nationalists.

Under Chandrika Kumaratunga's leadership, the Sri Lankan Parliament lifted an embargo against the Jaffna Peninsula. As prime minister, Kumaratunga began discussing peace with the Tamil Tigers, but she couldn't carry much weight in such talks. The post of prime minister in

Acting President Dingiri Banda Wijetunga in May 1993.

dent Wijetunge, was no longer supported by the majority of the country's legislators. The People's Alliance chose the SLFP's leader, Chandrika Kumaratunga, to be prime minister.

Kumaratunga was the daughter of two former prime ministers—SWRD Bandaranaike and Sirimavo Bandaranaike—and Sri Lanka's political violence had deeply touched her life. At the age of 13, she watched as a Sinhalese extremist murdered her father. In 1988 she was at home when a gunman drove his motorcycle into the driveway and killed her husband, Vijaya Kumaratunga—a popular movie star and politician whose views were

After the People's Alliance edged out the UNP in the August 1994 parliamentary elections, SLFP leader Chandrika Kumaratunga became the alliance's candidate for president.

Sri Lanka is far less powerful than that of president, the position for which she ran in the 1994 November election. Kumaratunga eventually won, but the campaign was marred by another assassination—of her main opponent, Gamini Dissanayake, whom the UNP had nominated for president.

For the first time since 1977—when J. R. Jayewardene and the UNP defeated Sirimavo Bandaranaike—the UNP was out of power and the SLFP was in. Kumaratunga was president and Bandaranaike, Kumaratunga's mother, was again appointed prime minister.

Kumaratunga started formal peace talks with the Tigers in January 1995. With hopes for some sort of settlement again running high, she went to Paris in April to

After the 1994 national elections were completed, Chandrika Kumaratunga (left) became president, and her mother, Sirimavo Bandaranaike (right), was named prime minister.

urge international aid donors such as the World Bank to invest more money in Sri Lanka. They said they were eager to do so, but only if peace could be achieved. By this time, the war had drained Sri Lanka's economy so badly that most Sri Lankans seemed willing to make peace with the Tamil Tigers.

THE TALKING STOPS

In April 1995, after explosives planted by Sea Tiger divers blew up two Sri Lankan navy ships in Trincomalee, the peace talks collapsed. The Tigers walked out, clearly intent on renewed fighting. One of the war's bloodiest phases then began. The war between the government and the Tamil separatists has claimed between 36,000 and 50,000 victims since 1983. From April

Reuters/Anuruddha Lokuhapuarachchi/Archive Photos

Preparing for the worst, government soldiers pledged their willingness to go to war against the LTTE if talks between the government and the Tigers failed. A month later, in April 1995, the Tigers renewed their attacks and ended the negotiations.

During the intense fighting of July 1995, government troops gathered the bodies of Tamil Tiger guerrillas after an LTTE attack on army bases in the northeast was thwarted.

through November of 1995 alone, about 4,000 soldiers, guerrillas, and civilians died.

In July 1995, the government launched Operation Leap Forward, an offensive intended to regain control of parts of the Jaffna Peninsula and to relieve pressure on government bases there. Soldiers at bases such as Palaly, surrounded by Tiger-held territory, sometimes felt like prisoners, as the Tigers shot down planes trying to enter or leave the base and ambushed patrols near the base's perimeters. Operation Leap Forward succeeded in giving government troops

there a bit more space, but it came nowhere near capturing Jaffna from the Tigers.

While it pursued a military hard line, the government proposed a political solution in July 1995. This was a plan for the **devolution** of power in Sri Lanka—the granting of increased authority to local units of government, such as the district councils. A more controversial provision was to redraw the borders of Sri Lanka's provinces and to turn the nation into a "union of regions," a collection of largely self-governing areas with ties to a far-weaker central government in Colombo.

This plan would give the Tamils more control over their own affairs without actually forming an independent country.

The Tamil Tigers quickly rejected the plan and vowed to keep fighting. In one highly publicized incident in early September 1995, the Tigers hijacked the *Iris Mona*, a ferry run by the Eelam People's Democratic Party (EPDP), a rival separatist group that had renounced violence. The 136 passengers, all Tamils, were held hostage for several days until the rebels released 121 of them. The Tigers held on to the remaining passengers and crew, perhaps as hostages to trade for rebel commandos being held by police.

Radical Sinhalese groups like the JVP also denounced the union of regions plan as an attempt to split up the country and hinted at another Sinhalese uprising to keep the plan from happening. Other Sinhalese groups said that they might accept devolution, but only after the Tamil Tigers had been crushed by the military. Moderate Tamil groups reacted positively, saying that the plan offered some hope for a settlement of the country's troubles. Before any part of the plan could be implemented, however, the Sri Lankan Parliament would have to approve big changes to the constitution.

THE GOVERNMENT MOVES IN

Meanwhile, the government launched another huge military push, Operation Sun Ray, on October 17, 1995. This maneuver was designed

Flanked by a bodyguard, Sivagnanam Karikalan—a regional LTTE leader—swore in a November 1995 press conference that the Tigers would not give up the city of Jaffna without a serious fight.

Reuters/Jason Reed/Archive Photos

as the final move to root the Tigers out of Jaffna. An unprecedented number of troops were assigned to the operation.

Pushing forward fast, the troops captured many key Tiger installations in towns just outside Jaffna, including Neervali, where they discovered an underground hospital and some airforce facilities.

Much of the territory they crossed was extensively booby-trapped by the fleeing Tigers. On November 20, a special unit of the government's best troops captured Nallur, a section in the eastern part of Jaffna city and the site of a major Hindu temple. About 2,000 soldiers, guerrillas, and civilians died in the first month of Operation Sun Ray.

Jaffna became a virtual ghost town as almost all its civilian residents fled to refugee camps in less-embattled areas east of the city. The Tigers who remained in Jaffna prepared to engage the government troops in house-to-house fighting that would result in very high casualties. The Tiger leader,

Reuters/Defence Ministry/Archive Photos

Government soldiers wait on alert while an elite reserve force entered Jaffna in November 1995.

Vellupillai Prab-hakaran, said that even if they were to lose their hold on Jaffna, they would continue to wage war from the jungle, as they had done after Indian troops took the city in 1988.

At the same time, the Tigers stepped up their attacks on villages in eastern Sri Lanka, killing civilians and burning the villages. The Tigers also sent waves of suicide bombers into Colombo, striking hotels, banks, government offices, shopping districts, and oil-storage facilities.

On December 2, 1995, government troops captured the symbolically important old Dutch fort in Jaffna and proclaimed themselves in control of the city. Sporadic sniping and ambushes demonstrated that the Tigers had not been completely driven from town, but for all practical purposes, Operation Sun Ray had succeeded. Immediately, President Kumaratunga offered amnesty

Dinodia Picture Agency

Above: *Tamil refugees clamored for food as they waited out the fighting on the Jaffna Peninsula. Unable to farm or conduct business during the war, thousands of Tamils were forced to leave their homes and seek shelter in refugee camps.* Right: *Residents of Boatta, in eastern Sri Lanka, fled to a makeshift shelter in a school after a Tamil Tiger attack on their village in November 1995.*

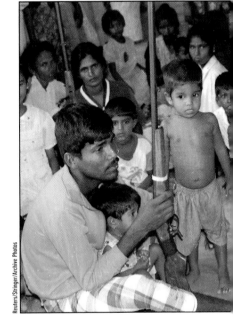

Reuters/Stringer/Archive Photos

(official pardon) to the Tamil Tigers and urged those residents who had fled their Jaffna homes to return and help rebuild the city.

The Tigers scoffed at the amnesty offer. Most of the Tamils remained in refugee camps, which were in parts of the Jaffna Peninsula still under Tiger control. By capturing Jaffna, the government inconvenienced the Tigers but did not finish them off. The Tigers still held huge chunks of territory, including most of the main part of the island north of Vavuniya.

With the success of Operation Sun Ray, those who wanted a military solution to Sri Lanka's problem seemed to be getting their way. But President Kumaratunga warned that the country could not afford a purely military solution. In April 1996, she said that the army would have to be doubled before it had any hope of crushing the Tigers. A military buildup of that extent, Kumaratunga continued, the country could not afford. She advocated searching for a political—not

Reuters/Defence Ministry/Archive Photos

Tamil civilians returned to the Jaffna Peninsula in April 1996, after fighting between government troops and the Tamil Tigers subsided. Here, a family passes through a government checkpoint.

Chandrika Kumaratunga addresses the press in July 1996. The same month, a suicide bomber in Jaffna attempted to kill the minister of construction, who was in charge of rebuilding the region.

Meanwhile Kumaratunga continued to push for negotiations and political changes in the effort to end the conflict with the LTTE.

©Dominic Sansoni/Panos Pictures

military—solution to the troubles that wouldn't go away.

As political solutions to Sri Lanka's conflict remained distant, the fighting persisted. In July 1996, an onslaught of 4,000 Tamil rebels overtook a military base in the north, surprising the 1,200 government troops stationed there. In 1997, an end to the long war in Sri Lanka still remained far out of reach. ⊕

4

WHAT'S BEING DONE TO SOLVE THE PROBLEM

Even if the Sri Lankan government managed to crush the Tamil Tigers, it would not mean the end of the nation's troubles. Military operations can deal with some of the symptoms of a country's ethnic conflict. But short of killing off most members of an ethnic community, warfare cannot end it. Other efforts—some by the government, some by international groups, and others by Sri Lanka's ordinary citizens—hold the only hope of getting at the roots of the problem.

WHAT THE GOVERNMENT CAN DO

The Sri Lankan government has the power to eliminate the sense among Tamils, Muslims, and other minorities that the system is stacked against them. The 1988 constitutional amendment making Tamil an official language, equal to Sinhala, was one important move. A similar action might be to amend the constitution so that all religions enjoy equal status. But this would certainly anger vast numbers of Buddhists, while pleasing only moderate numbers of Hindus, Christians, and Muslims. As long as most Sinhalese resist the separation of religion and government, the religious issue will be hard to solve.

Issues like religion indicate that **regional autonomy**—with different rules for different groups in different places—might be Sri Lanka's only reasonable course of action. This is what some specialists call the territorial management of ethnic conflict—defusing conflict by setting up viable divisions of territory. If, for example, Buddhism was officially the foremost religion only in overwhelmingly Buddhist districts, fewer people would be annoyed by the provision. **Federalism**—the distribution of power from national to regional and local authorities—is not a new idea in Sri Lanka, having been proposed in various forms since 1958. President Kumaratunga's devolution plan may have better luck than earlier ones simply because the nation, so weary of war, may now be ready for it.

Still, opposition by countless groups—from Sinhalese nationalists to Tamil rebels—threatens the devolution plan. Also, the question remains of how the borders of any new autonomous regions would be drawn. Will disputed areas like Vavuniya or Amparai fall into a Sinhalese-dominated region or a Tamil-dominated one? No matter how the lines are drawn, there will be minorities who would prefer to be part of the region next door. Subregions might wind up fighting to secede from one region to join another.

The government will also have to take a hard look at education policies. If universities continue to use ethnic **quotas** in admitting students, well-qualified Tamils will continue to be angry about being rejected so less-qualified Sinhalese students can attend.

On the other hand, the Sinhalese will not want to lose the quota system. They feel—justifiably or not—that the Tamils enjoyed unfair educational advantages in the past, and the Sinhalese need prefer-

ential treatment to catch up. Because higher education carries a lot of prestige, a compromise will be hard to reach.

Related to education is the issue of jobs. Although the Tamils make up 18 percent of the population, they hold less than 12 percent of all civil service jobs and less than 16 percent of administrative jobs. The Tamils do not dominate Sri Lanka's civil service, but many Sinhalese believe

they do. Yielding to Tamils a greater share of government jobs is likely to look like an unfair preference for Tamils, something the Sinhalese would resist. Nevertheless, the government has to find some way to give Tamils more stake in the everyday operation of the government.

Less controversially, the government could increase the proportion of Tamils and other minorities in the security forces. In 1987 Tamils

Government soldiers disabled in the war against the Tamil Tigers play a soccer game in a sports meet organized by the Sri Lankan military in April 1996. At that time, about 1,000 government soldiers had lost legs in the conflict by stepping on land mines.

Reuters/Anuruddha Lokuhapuarachchi/Archive Photos

made up about 5 percent of the police force and were almost absent from the armed services—only about 2 percent of the total. As older Tamil officers retire and as the forces recruit very few young Tamils, Tamil representation continues to decrease. To have an almost entirely Sinhalese army marching against Tamil areas is divisive and inflammatory. A proposal to set up a Tamil regiment in the army was made in August 1995 by the EPDP, and President Kumaratunga reportedly liked the idea. If the war drags on much longer, the ethnic mixture of the army may change forcibly as a result of a military draft, which would affect all young Sri Lankans.

The general lack of jobs in a hobbled economy is a serious problem for all ethnic groups. The unemployment rate was estimated at 15 percent in 1991 and has probably gotten worse since then. If the war ended, a huge weight would be lifted from a country that, by some accounts, spends about 25 percent of its tax revenues to fight its own citizens. But a vast amount of foreign investment would still be

"Those Days"

The wedding was taking place in Singapore, at the Sri Lankan High Commission (embassy) on the thirteenth floor of an office tower. Neither the groom—a young Tamil working in Denmark—nor the bride—a young Tamil from Jaffna—lived anywhere near Singapore. But the family knew it was safer to schedule the wedding in this busy city-state than for the groom to risk going back to Jaffna, a city full of traps for a young man of fighting age.

Had he returned to meet his bride in her home city, the groom might have had a lot of trouble getting out again, past Tiger watchdogs and suspicious government troops, to resume his work in Denmark. As it was, the young man had been able to fly to Singapore from Europe in eight hours, whereas it had taken the bride and her family six days to get there from Jaffna.

The Sri Lankan diplomat who conducted the wedding was a young Sinhalese man. He read them their vows—which they repeated slowly, tentatively, and not always exactly—in English. (English had been chosen because the diplomat didn't speak Tamil and the couple would not have wanted the ceremony done in Sinhala.)

Meanwhile, the bride's uncles and brothers zoomed in on the couple, the groom in a suit with arms a bit too long

Members of the International Red Cross unload food and supplies from a ship landed on the Jaffna Peninsula. The goods were distributed to Jaffna refugees.

and the bride in a beautiful brocade sash and gilt tiara, with camcorders large and small. The vows were said, rings were exchanged, and the couple—followed by their proud relatives—left the conference room that had served as their wedding chapel.

On impulse, the diplomat stopped a short, white-haired Tamil man, an uncle of the bride, on his way out of the wedding room. The diplomat guessed correctly that the older man—having lived part of his life under British rule—might be able to speak English.

"What did you do in those days?" asked the diplomat. The older man responded that he had worked for the government, and the two joked for a few moments about government work. Then the old uncle hurried out of the room to join the wedding party.

There was never any doubt about what the young diplomat meant by "those days." The phrase has a special meaning in Sri Lankan English. It means the time before everything fell apart, before a nation polarized so badly that a young Tamil man working in Denmark was better off hauling his fiancee's family to Singapore for a wedding than going home to Jaffna. The phrase carries a wistful tone, the implication of something good gone forever.

needed to create enough jobs in Sri Lanka for all the well-educated people who want to work. With one of the few economies in South Asia that hasn't yet boomed, Sri Lanka could attract investments but only if peace comes.

OUTSIDE PRESSURE

Sri Lanka's need for investment and aid from other countries puts worldwide pressure on the government to solve its problems. Not only are businesses afraid to set up where they might soon be burned out, but aid donors such as the World Bank do not want to invest money in an unstable country.

Groups that help refugees—primarily the offices the United Nations High

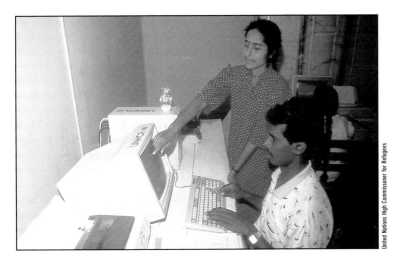

Tamil civilians who in 1990 had fled to Tamil Nadu in southern India returned home to Sri Lanka with help from the United Nations High Commissioner for Refugees. The organization provided medical assistance, loans, job training, and other resources to the refugees.

Two Peace Brigades volunteers accompany election monitors at a voting station in Batticaloa. PBI strives to help people feel safe in doing work they feel is dangerous because of the ethnic conflict in Sri Lanka.

Commissioner for Refugees and at the International Red Cross—have long been active in Sri Lanka. They became even more involved when most of Jaffna's population was displaced. The Sri Lankan government has often accused these groups of being too pro-Tamil and has tried to restrict their activities. But international opinion—and the need to care for hundreds of thousands of homeless people—forces the government to tolerate such groups and to accept international scrutiny.

Another form of international pressure comes from human-rights groups, such as Asia Watch and Amnesty International. These organizations closely examine the government's military moves, keeping an eye out for excessive force or the violation of civil rights. In Sri Lanka, these groups have been very interested in what went on during the death-squad days of the late 1980s.

Organizations such as Peace Brigades International (PBI) work in Sri Lanka to help conflicting groups negotiate peace without fearing for their safety. Since 1989 unarmed PBI members have accompanied civilians whose lives or safety have been threatened. By volunteering their presence alongside a person in danger, the PBI has deterred any would-be attackers from detaining or killing the individual. PBI also produces regular reports on human rights in Sri Lanka.

GRASSROOTS EFFORTS
After so much war, in which so many families have suffered, Sri Lanka's worst problems involve not just systems but attitudes—heartfelt distrust between ethnic groups, greed for land and good jobs, blood feuds going back many generations,

the notion that Sri Lanka belongs solely to Sinhalese Buddhists. Governments are good at changing rules, but not so good at changing hearts. If Sri Lanka's most basic problems are to be solved, ordinary Sri Lankans are going to have to be involved.

One group of Sri Lankan citizens trying to patch up the rifts between ethnic communities is the Sarvodaya Shramadana Movement of Sri Lanka. Based in the town of Moratuwa, just south of Colombo, this group promotes nonviolent resolution of conflict and looks for ways to bring together people of different backgrounds. For example, they have organized multiethnic hikes to the top of Adam's Peak, which Buddhists, Hindus, Muslims, and Christians alike consider holy. This shared reverence makes the peak a focus for unity among Sri Lankans.

Sarvodaya has also organized building projects in which Tamils, Sinhalese, and Muslims get together to repair damaged houses and buildings or improve the basic infrastructure of villages. In such projects, Sarvodaya is following the contact principle of conflict resolution, putting into place the idea that trust can be built by bringing together people who would otherwise distrust one another from afar.

Another group dedicated to bringing Sri Lankans together is the Marga Institute, based in Colombo. The institute is helping the United Nations Educational, Scientific, and Cultural Organization (UNESCO) carry out a program in which people from different ethnic

Dr. A. T. Ariyaratne (at right) *runs the Sarvodaya Shramadana Movement of Sri Lanka, which leads many projects that bring together Sri Lankans of different ethnic groups.*

communities plan and enact projects to improve basic village services—water, health care, sanitation, and so on. Marga also maintains an information service on the Internet, which they use to publicize plans that might promote peace in Sri Lanka. For example, they used their Internet site to distribute a five-page analysis of the devolution plan proposed by President Kumaratunga in 1995.

Other grassroots organizations—those run by ordinary citizens, not official governmental groups—have been working for peace in Sri Lanka. One, the Sri Lanka Association for Rehabilitating Villages, is a group that pairs Sinhalese villages with Tamil villages to work on village-improvement projects.

The Satyodaya Centre for Social Research and Encounter, based in Kandy, works to improve conditions among some of Sri Lanka's poorest and least-influential people, the Indian Tamils of the highlands. Other peace-promoting groups include the Non-Violent Direct Action Group (based in Chavakachcheri near Jaffna) and the Women's International League for Peace and Freedom.

Even among the worst accounts of violence in the riots of 1983 were stories of brave

> *Some Sri Lankans, even after all they have been through, can still stop being primarily Sinhalese or Tamil or Muslim or Burgher or Vedda long enough to be just one person helping another.*

Sinhalese families risking their homes, or even their lives, to shelter their Tamil neighbors from the rampaging crowds. Barbara Crossette wrote in the *New York Times* of a retired military man giving up his well-earned rest to patch up rifts in communities. She also chronicled the work of a Buddhist abbot who drives

A poster in Kandy reminds Sri Lankans of the damage that war can do. Many thousands of children have lost parents in the Sinhalese-Tamil conflict.

These Tamil children, displaced by the war, were taken into a shelter in Batticaloa. The aid agency Terre des Hommes started an experimental program there, putting together makeshift families.

from settlement to settlement mediating disputes and helping people in trouble.

Author William McGowan tells of Father Eugene Herbert, a Jesuit priest working near Batticaloa who disappeared while trying to help Muslims whose village had been attacked. Maybe certain ungrateful Muslims, who had a record of attacking priests, got him. Maybe it was the government security forces. As is common in Sri Lanka, it's difficult to know what happened, why it happened, and who did it.

But even in group-crazy Sri Lanka, brave individuals make a difference. Some Sri Lankans, even after all they have been through, can still stop being primarily Sinhalese or Tamil or Muslim or Burgher or Vedda long enough to be just one person helping another. They stand in contrast to the spirit that brought trouble to the island in the first place and then kept it alive—a perversion of group identity, a belief that one's ethnic, religious, or linguistic group matters more than one's basic humanity.

These individuals also offer the strongest evidence that the count of war dead may eventually freeze, that the bus stations and marketplaces might stop exploding, that villagers may no longer be dragged from their beds and murdered, that people might finally be able to go back home and live in peace. ⊕

EPILOGUE*

After 15 years of conflict and more than 50,000 war-related deaths, most Sri Lankans have resigned themselves to more fighting. President Kumaratunga's proposed constitutional reforms, which would give autonomy to the predominantly Tamil North-Eastern Province, have been rejected by the LTTE and have been held up in committee by President Kumaratunga's opponents in the government. With no viable political solution, the government has continued to use military force to try to squelch the Tamil Tigers.

Local elections held in March 1997 demonstrated that the Sri Lankan people continued to support the People's Alliance and President Kumaratunga's peace-process initiatives. By most accounts, the elections were carried out fairly and without violence.

As of spring 1997, the Sri Lankan government still occupied Jaffna city, but government military bases on the Jaffna Peninsula continued to suffer frequent attacks by Tiger guerrillas. The Tigers controlled about 10 percent of the island and maintained about 25 percent of it as zones off limits to government troops. Nonetheless, the government launched yet another offensive—Operation Brave Force—in the north. Meanwhile, LTTE guerrillas overran more military bases, capturing enormous stockpiles of weapons.

*Please note: The information presented in *Sri Lanka: War-Torn Island* was current at the time of the book's publication. For the most up-to-date information on the conflict in Sri Lanka, you may want to look for articles in the *Far Eastern Economic Review*, which is published weekly. You may also wish to access, via the Internet, two newspapers published in English in Sri Lanka: *Daily News* and *Sunday Observer*, at http://www.lanka.net/lakehouse. Another Internet resource is the Sri Lankan Information Centre's LankaWeb page at http://www.lankaweb.com/news/.

CHRONOLOGY

ca. 500 BC   Sinhalese migrate from India to Sri Lanka, where they develop a civilization based on irrigated farming. They build a capital at Anuradhapura.

ca. 200 BC   Buddhism spreads through Sri Lanka.

ca. AD 1000   Successive invasions from southern India force the Sinhalese kingdom to move southward.

ca. 1200   Tamils establish a kingdom called Jaffnapatnam in the north.

1505   The Portuguese land on Sri Lanka, eventually seizing control of much of the island.

1658   The Dutch overcome the Portuguese and take control of Sri Lanka.

1796   The British force the Dutch out of Sri Lanka.

1802   The British declare Sri Lanka a British colony called Ceylon.

1815   The British conquer Kandy, bringing all of Sri Lanka under British rule. The British set up a plantation system on the island.

1948   Sri Lanka regains its independence, becoming a free nation.

1948-49   Sri Lankan legislature declares the Estate Tamils non-citizens of Sri Lanka.

1956   The 2,500th anniversary of the Buddha's death. Pro-Sinhalese sentiment led to the Sinhala-Only Act, which made Sinhalese the only official language and the only language to be used in any governmental affairs.

1958   In protest of the finalized Sinhala-Only Act, Tamils protest and are attacked by Sinhalese mobs. Violent ethnic riots cause many injuries and deaths, and thousands of Tamils flee north to the Jaffna Peninsula.

1959   Prime Minister SWRD Bandaranaike is assassinated by a Buddhist monk opposed to any reforms that would accommodate Tamils.

1960   Sirimavo Bandaranaike becomes prime minister after her husband's death.

1964   India and Sri Lanka reach an agreement over Sri Lanka's stateless Indian Tamils. Each country agrees to grant citizenship to a proportion of the 1.1 million Indian Tamils. The process is slated to begin in 1968.

1965   The UNP, under Prime Minister Dudley Senanayke, returns to power. Senanayke agrees to some Tamil concessions, restoring the use of the Tamil language in government in Tamil-dominated areas and limiting Sinhalese colonization of the north and east.

1966   Massive Sinhalese demonstrations, led by the JVP, take place in protest to the Tamil concessions.

1968   The process awarding citizenship to Sri Lanka's Indian Tamils takes place, but only 225,000 out of more than 700,000 were granted the Sri Lankan citizenship they requested.

1970   Sirimavo Bandaranaike returns to power, leading a coalition group that includes the SLFP and several other left-wing parties.

1971   The JVP instigates massive rioting, aiming to overthrow the government.

1972   The government approves a new constitution, officially changing the nation's name from Ceylon to Sri Lanka. The constitution declares Buddhism to hold special status, institutionalizes Sinhalese as the official language, and ignores demands for Tamil autonomy. Radical Tamils found the LTTE.

1977   The UNP wins elections, and Junius Jayawardene becomes prime minister.

1978 The constitution is amended, creating the powerful post of president, to which Jayawardene is elected. The country's official name becomes the Democratic Socialist Republic of Sri Lanka. Sinhalese remains the official language, although Tamil receives recognition as a national tongue.

1979 Civil unrest in Jaffna results in the government declaring a state of emergency there. The government also passes the Prevention of Terrorism Act.

1981 Unrest spreads throughout Sri Lanka.

1983 Unrest becomes widespread rioting. The violence results in the mass destruction of homes and businesses in Colombo. Thousands of Tamils are killed or injured, and thousands more flee to the Jaffna Peninsula or to India.

1985 As violence continues, political tensions mount between Sri Lanka and India. Jayawardene announces plans to settle 200,000 Sinhalese in the northern and eastern Tamil provinces.

1986 Government offensive in the north and east results in all-out warfare between government forces and Tamil guerrillas. The government grants citizenship to 233,000 more of the stateless Indian Tamils.

1987 The LTTE takes control of the administration of the Jaffna Peninsula, and the Sri Lankan government retaliates with an economic blockade. India becomes directly involved in the conflict, securing an agreement with Sri Lanka that provides for a devolution of power in the Tamil provinces. The Indian Peace-Keeping Force arrives in the north.

1988 As fighting continues in the north, JVP-led strikes and riots disrupt life on the rest of the island. The Sri Lankan government approves the temporary merger of the northern and eastern Tamil provinces into the North-Eastern Province. Ranasinghe Premadasa, leader of the UNP, wins the presidential election.

1989 The LTTE and the Sri Lankan government hold negotiations. Indian forces begin to pull out from the north. A government offensive against the JVP results in the capture and killing of the group's top leaders.

1990 The last of the Indian troops withdraw from Sri Lanka. Thousands of Tamils also flee the North-Eastern Province, and fighting resumes between the LTTE and government forces.

1991 Indian Prime Minister Rajiv Gandhi is assassinated in Tamil Nadu, India. The LTTE is suspected to be responsible.

1993 Sri Lankan President Ranasinghe Premadasa is assassinated. The LTTE is again blamed.

1994 Elections bring to power the People's Alliance, a coalition that includes the SLFP. The SLFP leader, Chandrika Kumaratunga, becomes president, and her mother, Sirimavo Bandaranaike, becomes prime minister.

1995 Kumaratunga initiates peace talks with the LTTE. The peace talks collapse when the LTTE resumes attacks. The war escalates.

1996 Heavy fighting continues on the Jaffna Peninsula.

1997 Local elections reaffirm the voters' support of the coalition government led by Kumaratunga.

SELECTED BIBLIOGRAPHY

De Silva, K. M., *Managing Ethnic Tensions in Multiethnic Societies: Sri Lanka 1880–1985*. Lanham, 1986.

Manor, James, ed. *Sri Lanka in Change and Crisis*. London: Croom Helm, 1984.

McGowan, William, *Only Man is Vile*. New York: Farrar, Strauss and Giroux, 1992.

Ross, Russell R. and Andrea M. Savada, eds. *Sri Lanka: A Country Study*. Washington: U.S. Government Printing Office, 1990.

Ryan, Stephen, *Ethnic Conflict and International Relations*. Aldershot (U.K.): Dartmouth Publishing, 1995.

Spencer, Jonathan, ed. *Sri Lanka: History and the Roots of Conflict*. London: Routledge, 1990.

Tambiah, S. J., *Sri Lanka: Ethnic Fratricide and the Dismantling of Democracy*. Chicago: University of Chicago Press, 1986.

Wilson, A. Jeyaratnam, "Ethnic Strife in Sri Lanka: The Politics of Space." In *The Territorial Management of Ethnic Conflict*, edited by John Coakley. London: Frank Cass & Co, 1993.

Wimalaratne, K. D. G., *Directory of Dates and Events: Sri Lanka (Ceylon) (543 B.C. – 1984 A.D.)*. Colombo: Trumpet Publishers, 1988.

INDEX

Adam's Peak, 10, 12, 87
Amnesty International, 33, 86
Amparai, 23, 29, 53, 71, 83
Anuradhapura, 35, 36–37, 38, 58
Asia Watch, 86
Asoka, 35
assassinations and murders, 25–28, 33, 58–60, 67–69, 72–74, 76, 79
Athulathmudali, Lalith, 67
Bandaranaike, Sirimavo, 20, 55, 56, 65, 68, 73, 74
Bandaranaike, Solomon West Ridgeway Dias (SWRD), 20, 21, 52, 53–54, 55, 73
Batticaloa, 13, 23, 24, 29, 71, 89
Blavatsky, Helena Petrovna, 48
Britain, 15, 36, 40–46, 48–49, 51
British Special Air Service, 27
Buddha (Siddhartha Gautama), 10, 14, 34, 35, 42
Buddhism, 14–15, 17, 18, 29, 35–43, 51, 55, 57, 65, 82; revival of, 46–48
caste systems, 15, 17, 39, 46
Central Bank, 27
Ceylon, 40, 44, 46, 48–49, 50, 51
Ceylon Tamils, 15, 45–46
Chola, 37–38
Christianity, 15, 17, 40
cities. See Colombo; Jaffna
Colombo, 13, 40, 68, 76, 87; population of, 13; violence in, 18, 19, 25, 27, 29, 31, 48, 53–55, 57–60, 63–65, 79
colonialism, 15, 17–18, 29, 39–46, 67
Crossette, Barbara, 88
death squads, 31, 33, 68, 69, 86
Dehiwala–Mount Lavinia, 13
demonstrations, 53, 54, 56
Devanampiyatissa, 34, 35
Dharmapala, Anagarika, 20, 47–48, 52
disappeared, 33, 58, 68, 89
Dissanayake, Gamini, 25, 74
D'Orly, John, 42–43
Duriappah, Alfred, 63
Duttugamunu, 37
education, 18–19, 56, 83
Eelam, 21, 25, 28, 51, 62
Eelam National Democratic Liberation Front (ENDLF), 20
Eelam People's Democratic Party, 84
Eelam People's Revolutionary Liberation Front, 69, 76
Eelam Revolutionary Organization of Students, 63
Elara, 37
elections, 25, 68–69, 72–75

Estate Tamils. See Indian Tamils
ethnic groups, 13–17, 18, 29. See also Muslims; Sinhalese; Tamils
federalism, 82
Galle, 13, 40
Gal Oya, 29
Gamanayake, Upatissa, 69
Gandhi, Rajiv, 30, 64–65, 72
George VI, King, 49
guerrilla warfare, 23, 29, 30–33, 58, 61–63, 68–69, 71, 76, 78
Hamangoda, Ananda, 28
Herbert, Eugene, 89
Hinduism, 14, 15, 17, 36, 39, 46–48
history, 35–40; British period, 40–46; independence movement, 48–49; religious revivals, 46–48
Home Guards, 31
homeless, 61, 86
independence movement, 48–49
India, 10, 13–15, 20, 31, 37–40, 58, 63–67, 71, 72
Indian Peace Keeping Force (IPKF), 20, 65, 67
Indian Tamils, 15, 39, 45–46, 50, 63, 88
Indo–Sri Lankan Agreement, 64–65
International Red Cross, 84, 86
Jaffna, 13, 27–28, 38, 40, 58–59, 61, 71, 78–80, 86; population of, 13; refugee camps in, 22, 24, 78, 80
Jaffna Lagoon, 23, 38
Jaffnapatnam, 38
Jaffna Peninsula, 10, 22, 26, 29, 61, 63, 64, 71, 73, 76, 80
Janatha Vimukthi Peramuna (JVP), 20, 30–31, 33, 55–56, 67, 68–69, 71, 77
Jayewardene, Junius Richard, 21, 30, 56–57, 59, 60, 63–64, 67, 68, 74
jobs, 18–19, 44–45. See also unemployment
Kallawara, 26
Kandy, 13, 40–43, 88
Knuckles Massif, 12
Kotahena, 48
Kotte, 13, 38
Kumaratunga, Chandrika, 29, 32, 33, 55, 73–74, 79–81, 82, 84, 88
Kumaratunga, Vijaya, 68, 73
languages, 14–15, 17, 19, 53, 65. See also Sinhala; Tamil (language)
Liberation Tigers of Tamil Eelam (LTTE), 22–33, 37, 60, 62–63, 67, 69–80; definition of, 21; formation of, 57; guerrillas, 30–33, 61–63, 68–69, 71, 76, 78; killings by, 25–28, 63, 67, 71, 72–77
Liyanarachchi, Wijedasa, 68

Madras, 62
Mahanama, 36
Mahavamsa, 36–37, 47, 48, 57
Mahaweli Ganga, 12
Mannar, 40, 58
Marga Institute, 87–88
McGowan, William, 89
Moratuwa, 13, 87
Mother's Front, 33
Muslims, 13, 16, 17, 23, 29, 39, 46, 48, 89
Nallur, 78
nationalism, 37, 47–48, 51–52, 58, 64, 73, 82
Navali, 26
Neervali, 78
Negombo, 40
Netherlands, 40
Non–Violent Direct Action Group, 88
North–Eastern Province, 13, 17, 20, 29, 55, 67, 68–69,
    71
Olcott, Henry Steel, 48
Operation Leap Forward, 76
Operation Sun Ray, 77–78, 79, 80
Palaly, 32, 76
Panduvasaveda, 35
Peace Brigades International (PBI), 86
peace negotiations, 26, 30–33, 71, 73, 74–75, 86
People's Alliance, 72–73
Polonnaruwa, 38
Pooneryn, 23
population, 13
Portugal, 39–40
Prabhakaran, Vellupillai, 21, 28, 62–63, 65, 67, 72, 79
Premadasa, Ranashinge, 21, 67, 68–69, 71, 72
protests, nonviolent. *See* demonstrations
provinces, 13, 18, 63. *See also* North–Eastern Province
rebel groups. *See* Janatha Vimukthi Peramuna (JVP);
    Liberation Tigers of Tamil Eelam (LTTE)
refugee camps, 22, 64, 65, 78, 79–80
refugees, 61, 63, 64, 79, 85
religion, 46–48. *See also* Buddhism; Hinduism; Islam
riots, 18, 19, 48, 53–56, 58, 59–61, 65
Rohana, 37
Sarvodaya Shramadana Movement of Sri Lanka, 87
Satyodaya Centre for Social Research and Encounter, 88
Sea Tigers, 25, 75
secession, 20, 21, 28, 29
Senanayake, Don Stephen, 21, 50
separatism, 25, 28, 31, 51, 55–58, 61–62, 63, 64,
    75–76. *See also* Liberation Tigers of Tamil Eelam
    (LTTE)

Sinhala, 13, 35, 36, 39, 51, 52–55, 57, 65
Sinhalese, 12, 13–14, 17–18, 23, 28–33, 51–61, 64–65,
    67, 71, 77; easing ethnic tensions, 82–89; history of,
    35–40, 42, 47–48. *See also* Janatha Vimukthi
    Peramuna (JVP)
Special Task Force (STF), 27
Sri Jayewardenapura, 13
Sri Lanka: divisions, 13, 17; economic activities, 18–19;
    ethnic groups, 13–17, 18; landscape, 10–12; name,
    10, 51; rainfall, 12
Sri Lanka Association for Rehabilitating Villages, 88
Sri Lanka Freedom Party (SLFP), 20, 21, 52, 56, 65, 68,
    72–73, 74
Sri Pada. *See* Adam's Peak
suicide bombings, 26–28, 72
Tamil (language), 14, 16, 36, 39, 51, 52–53, 55, 57, 65,
    82
Tamil Nadu, 63, 72, 85
Tamils, 12, 13, 14–15, 17–18, 20, 51–72; easing ethnic
    tensions, 82–89; history of, 35–40, 48. *See also*
    Ceylon Tamils; Indian Tamils; Tamil Tigers
Tamil Tigers. *See* Liberation Tigers of Tamil Eelam
    (LTTE)
Tamil United Front (TUF), 21
Tamil United Liberation Front (TULF), 21, 55, 61, 62
terrorism. *See* guerrilla warfare
Trincomalee, 10, 13, 25–26, 29, 40, 75
unemployment, 70, 84–85
United National Party (UNP), 20, 21, 33, 50, 56–57,
    65, 68, 72, 74
United Nations Educational, Scientific, and Cultural
    Organization (UNESCO), 87
United Nations High Commissioner for Refugees,
    85–86
Upatissigama, 35
Vadamarachi, 62–63
Vanni, 24
Vavuniya, 22, 23, 24, 58, 80, 83
Veddas, 16, 35
Vijaya, 35, 36–37, 40
violence, 25–28, 29–30, 67. *See also* assassinations and
    murders; death squads; disappeared; guerrilla
    warfare; riots; suicide bombings
Wellawatte, 59
Wijetunge, Dingiri Banda, 72–73
Wijeweera, Rohana, 69
Women's International League for Peace and Freedom,
    88
World Bank, 75, 85

ABOUT THE AUTHOR

Lawrence J. Zwier is a writer, editor, and university lecturer who has lived and worked in Minnesota, Saudi Arabia, Malaysia, and Japan. He lives in Singapore with his wife and two children.

ABOUT THE CONSULTANTS

Andrew Bell-Fialkoff, *World in Conflict* series consultant, is a specialist on nationalism, ethnicity, and ethnic conflict. He is the author of *Ethnic Cleansing*, published by St. Martin's Press in 1996, and has written numerous articles for *Foreign Affairs* and other journals. He is currently writing a book on the role of migration in the history of the Eurasian Steppe. Bell-Fialkoff lives in Bradford, Massachusetts.

Marlene Krysl, Director of the Creative Writing Program at the University of Colorado in Boulder, has published hundreds of poems, stories, and essays in a number of books, anthologies, and journals including *The Atlantic*, *The Nation*, and *The New Republic*. She coedits the literary journal *Many Mountains Moving*. Krysl has worked as a volunteer for Peace Brigades International in Sri Lanka and has also worked in India and in China.